The A-Z of Curious Somerset

First published 2013

The History Press
The Mill, Brimscombe Port
Stroud, Gloucestershire, GL5 2QG
www.thehistorypress.co.uk

British Library Cataloguing in Publication Data.
A catalogue record for this book is available from the British Library.

ISBN 978 0 7524 9329 9

Typesetting and origination by The History Press
Printed in Great Britain

Introduction and Acknowledgements

Quite soon after I came to the West Country, more than half a lifetime ago, I realised what an incredible part of Britain was now on my doorstep. My first physical explorations of Somerset confirmed this impression, with even more fascinating discoveries coming to light from time spent in the Somerset Studies Library and the County Record Office at Taunton delving into the events and people that had shaped its history. I owe much to the staff in those places.

Hoping to share the fascination I was finding, I wrote a small book, *Exploring the Smaller Towns of Somerset*, half a dozen other works on diverse local subjects and a series of 'Town Trails' and other articles for the former *Somerset Magazine*. Roy Gallop was an invaluable partner in all these efforts.

This book dips into the files of information I have collected over the years and attempts to present a selection of some of the most unusual, intriguing and entertaining items they contain. Nicola Guy, Declan Flynn, and the staff of The History Press have, as always, been immensely helpful and supportive. Tess Green has generously contributed information on two subjects and my sister, Maureen Etheridge, has kindly cast a tutored eye over my efforts. To these, and the many past contributors to the 'Notes & Queries' columns of the *Somerset Herald* I have scrutinised, I am extremely grateful. Any shortcomings in the outcome of all this are entirely mine and are much regretted.

The illustrations are from my own collection, except where otherwise indicated.

A

ABBOT WHITING'S MARTYRDOM

In the year 1539 a sad drama came to its dramatic climax on the summit of Glastonbury Tor. The story had been building up for the best part of five years, over which period the consequences of King Henry VIII's break from the Church of Rome had become more and more apparent throughout England. Its size and importance had preserved Glastonbury Abbey for a time, but even such an eminent and well-run foundation could not escape the process of dissolving the monasteries which was yielding such riches for the monarch and those he favoured.

To justify the process there had to be scapegoats and, quite undeservedly, Glastonbury's abbot became one of these. Lord Russell, who was in charge of the affair, described the outcome in his subsequent report to Thomas Cromwell,

Although much of the former Glastonbury Abbey is now in ruins, the erstwhile Abbot's Kitchen conveys some idea of the splendid place it must once have been.

writing: 'that on Thursdaye the 14th daye of this moneth the Abbott of Glastonburye was arrayed, and the next daye putt to execution with two other of his monkes for the robbying of Glastonburye Churche, on the Torre Hyll next unto the towne of Glastonburye'.

The abbot referred to was Richard Whiting, a man of modest origins who had studied at Cambridge, been ordained priest and then given an appointment as chamberlain at Glastonbury's famous abbey. He seems to have attracted the favourable attention of Cardinal Wolsey who, in a surprise decision, elevated him to the highest position in that great religious establishment, that of abbot. Taking over in 1524, Abbot Whiting seems to have been an effective leader, carrying out the religious and pastoral duties of the abbey well, and effectively managing its large establishment, its great landownings and its many satellite houses. Forty-seven monks witnessed his election as abbot and supported the abbey's works with more piety and discipline than was apparent at some religious foundations.

Inevitably, all this was to change in the massive upheaval which followed Henry VIII's divorce from Queen Catherine of Aragon and his consequent break with the Pope and the Roman Catholic religion. Whatever Abbot Whiting's personal reservations about the king's chosen means of changing the nation's religious allegiance and practices, he duly appended his signature to the tool chosen for this, the 1534 Act of Supremacy. In the following year, Thomas Cromwell was appointed Vicar General and, interpreting the king's wishes, instigated a survey of England's religious houses. As a result of this, Glastonbury Abbey was inspected by Dr Richard Layton who reported that there was 'nothing notable' to say about it. It became increasingly clear later that Layton could not find any real fault with either Glastonbury or nearby Bruton.

The Act for the Submission of the Clergy and other legislation in the 1534 package was supplemented in 1535 by a statute governing the dissolution of the smaller monasteries. These were the simplest prey, and Cromwell's commissioners no doubt saw them as easy to find fault with and to relieve of their land and treasures. So began a process of pensioning off the inoffensive clergy and making an example of the obdurate, coupled with lining the pockets of the monarch and his chosen beneficiaries. Richard Whiting must have watched this process with growing concern and he tried to protect his own establishment by frequent gifts and written appeals to those with influence. To no avail.

Dr Layton appears to have felt that Abbot Whiting was a man without fault, which was not the direction in which his masters wanted to go. Some of the larger monasteries had already surrendered themselves voluntarily, and a 1539 Act legitimising this also gave powers to dissolve the remainder, especially if treason or any other crime was discovered. Whiting and his abbey were now doomed. On 7 April he wrote a pitiful letter to Cromwell arguing against a summons to London, pleading that for some time he had been 'greatlye diseased with dyvers infirmyties', but it failed to deter Cromwell, influenced not only by his monarch, also but by the amount of confiscated wealth rolling in.

Already the religious houses of the West Country had yielded up around 500 ounces of gold and 45,000 ounces of silver and silver plate, and there was more to be had at Glastonbury. More commissioners came down and began the authorised looting there, but the abbot appears to have been left alone until a surprise visit by a group of commissioners on 19 September 1535, when Whiting was told that the abbey would close. He was taken from his house at Sharpham and confined in his lodging at the abbey. He was soon escorted to London and there confronted with prepared charges, never fully disclosed, before being returned to Glastonbury under guard. The opportunity had been taken to search the abbot's personal possessions in his absence and damning evidence was allegedly 'discovered' in the process. Whether or not it had been conveniently planted there is a matter for conjecture.

Even less information was forthcoming about a trial of Abbot Whiting which was staged before a jury at Wells on 14 November, but certainly no effort had been spared by Cromwell's emissaries to extort damning testimonies against him from some who feared for their own safety. The outcome of the examination was certain and swift. The verdict 'condemned to death' was widely publicised, but there was no publicity for the trial evidence and process.

After being taken back to the abbey under escort and spending the night there, Richard Whiting, his treasurer John Thorne and the sub-treasurer Roger James were roused the next morning. The day was destined to be their last. In a sad and degrading spectacle the three unfortunates were placed upon hurdles which were dragged by horses up the steep slope to the summit of the tor.

The tower of the fourteenth-century church of St Michael, another victim of the Dissolution process, still stands on the top of Glastonbury Tor marking the spot where Abbot Whiting was put to death.

There, overlooking the abbey and its Somerset domain, Whiting, Thorne and James met their deaths.

In his letter of 16 November 1539 quoted at the beginning, Lord Russell continued: 'the seyde abbot's body being devyded into foure parts, and the hedde stryken off; whereof one quarter stondythe at Welles, another at Bathe and at Ylchester, and Brigewater the rest, and his hedde upon the Abbeygate at Glastonburye.'

More loads of looted treasure went up to London, the estates were sold off over a period of years and the 1,500 people managed by the abbey had to settle down to new masters and lifestyle. Fortunately the ruins of the abbey have survived and Abbot Whiting's life and service was honoured by his church with beatification in May 1895.

ABJURE THE REALM

The right of a wanted man to seek sanctuary in a church lasted in this country for a thousand years, and at one period, as many as 1,000 people would exercise this right in a typical year. Somerset had its share of these, with cases recorded at places as far apart as Watchet and Yeovil.

The tradition of sanctuary was well known to the Greeks and Romans and was formalised here by King Ethelbert in AD 600. It was perpetuated after the Norman Conquest, and in cases of felony those accused could surrender themselves at any consecrated church and be protected from their pursuers. Only a limited number of chartered sanctuaries could take in people wanted for treason, and there was no succour at all if sacrilege was involved.

So how did the right of sanctuary work? In the main, two classes of society made use of it. Noblemen involved in a blood feud, or some other dispute over wealth or power, might choose to seek sanctuary rather than risk being cut down by their rivals. More ordinary people, usually driven to theft by need or hunger, would only choose the sanctuary option if the law was hot on their heels, but might then consider it a lesser evil than risking the harsh punishments of their times.

Once the fugitive was on consecrated ground, usually denoted by the churchyard boundary, he was safe. The commotion of the chase would alert the priest or churchwarden to the situation and a bell would be rung to denote the granting of sanctuary.

The church and community had then to hold its visitor secure while the coroner was sent for and the unexpected, and probably unwelcome, arrival had been given the choice of surrendering to the law or remaining in sanctuary. If he chose the latter he had to swear to 'abjure the realm' within a stipulated period, ultimately extended to forty days, and never to return. If he escaped during the sanctuary period, the church and its parishioners could expect a severe penalty.

This recess in Chewton Mendip church is believed to be one of the few surviving examples of the seat which sanctuary seekers were obliged to use, sometimes known as a 'frith', or peace, stool.

At certain times, implementing the abjuration process involved stringent conditions, such as being forced to wear simple pilgrim garb and carry a small, symbolic wooden cross. The subject might choose his own port of embarkation, but had to follow a specific route and tarry no longer than a single night at any point on the journey. He was obliged to seek a ship immediately and, if a passage was not to be had, to wade into the sea each day and sleep on the beach each night. Failure to leave the country within the appointed time meant having to seek a renewal of sanctuary locally. Coupled with the automatic loss of property that went with this exile status, sanctuary was clearly not a soft option.

Not surprisingly, this ancient right of church protection sometimes caused friction with other parties involved. In 1318 Walter Brinton had no sooner grasped the sanctuary ring on the door of Chedzoy church than his pursuers dragged him away and carried him off to Somerton Gaol.

When news reached the bishop at Wells, he was incensed and insisted that Brinton be restored to Chedzoy as the right of sanctuary provided. Somerton then featured in another case in 1340, when one John Durburgh was on his way to Somerton to give evidence in a case against a member of the powerful de Mohun family. He was waylaid by a group of armed men and only just managed to reach the church there ahead of them. Despite claiming sanctuary, his pursuers dragged him out and set off along the road to Langport. Fortunately for Durburgh, the sheriff and a band of followers managed to rescue him and de Mohun was eventually imprisoned for his offence, subsequently receiving a royal pardon.

In the thirteenth and fourteenth centuries claims for sanctuary are recorded at a variety of places in Somerset including: Taunton; North Petherton; Yeovil; Martock; Bagborough; Stogumber; Ilton; Chedzoy; Crewkerne; Huish Episcopi; Ilchester; Stogursey; Somerton; and Watchet. The Watchet case of two murderers had two different outcomes; one fled and was outlawed and the other abjured the realm. At Yeovil in 1420 John Green, thought to be fleeing from a duelling death, was sent to Southampton but failed to keep his abjuration oath and was brought back for trial.

On the door of Chedzoy church a ring or knocker was once provided for use by anyone claiming sanctuary.

A most unusual case of people seeking sanctuary occurred at Ilchester in 1276. The church involved was St Olaves, which belonged to Montacute Priory. Its priest must have been astonished on the day when, according to one account, 'a thief removed from the gallows for burial in the churchyard, recovered and sought sanctuary there.'

After Henry VIII broke with Rome, the practice of sanctuary started to change. Not only did the state seek more control of the law, but churches proved less than keen on the burden of supporting sanctuary claimants. Eventually, special 'chartered sanctuary' status was accorded to just a small number of locations, Wells among them, but this brought them an influx of the sort of people they were not willing to welcome. James I, an astute and pragmatic monarch, then abolished the right of sanctuary in 1623 except for a few specific civil cases, mainly involving debt. Curiously the concept lingered on in a few places, and a Weston-super-Mare innkeeper is said to have lived on Steep Holm island for seven years, claiming it offered sanctuary and precluded proceedings being taken against him for debt.

ACROSS THE PARRETT

By the beginning of the present century an odd survivor of a once-important travellers' route stood alone, uninhabited and neglected, a little way from the eastern bank of the River Parrett opposite the village of Combwich. It was once a fairly substantial building, at times full of life and activity, but it fell into disuse; its walls crumbled and shrubs and brambles began to grow in profusion where once travellers had paused for refreshment.

The former road from Pawlett to the River Parrett and the site of the ferry across to Combwich with the site of the former *White House Inn* on its right.

This was the former White House Inn, probably so-called from being whitewashed to provide a progress marker for the vessels that plied along the adjacent river on their journey between Bridgwater and the open waters of the Bristol Channel.

This curious location for an inn is not so strange when a look at the map reveals that it lies on a direct 'crow-flight' line between the traditional road south from Bristol and a very large land area between the Quantock Hills and the Channel coast. The modern route lies via Bridgwater, but this adds a number of miles to the journey and this factor would have been of considerable significance in former times when most travellers had to make their journeys on foot. Even the use of horses meant strict limitations on the rate of progress. This choice of the route and river crossing would be even more understandable to present minds if the roadside through Pawlett still carried the old sign which pointed and read, 'To the Ferry'.

A ferryman is recorded at Combwich as early as 1327, but his boat was not the first route across the river. Starting from a point on the east bank, near where the ferry used to berth, there is a ridge of hard lias rock running diagonally beneath the river to the west bank. Although visible only when the water is at an unusually low level, this causeway provided a firm and shallow way for people and animals to cross the river, long before the ferry was introduced or Bridgwater got its first bridge. It was still crossed occasionally by farmers and other local people into

It is not easy to visualise trows and ketches bringing coal to this tiny pill for unloading and then sailing with a cargo of bricks or agricultural produce. The more recent structure was built as an unloading point for materials for the Hinckley Point nuclear power complex.

the twentieth century and a local comment records, 'The Combwich ford was well known and used in former days. It was the chief route to Glastonbury and Salisbury. At low tide horses and cattle were safely driven across the river.'

The tiny pill at Combwich was being used by small sailing vessels taking corn to Ireland and other markets as early as the fourteenth century. It continued to despatch local produce over the years, served as a base for larger vessels on longer routes, dealt with timber and other goods being transhipped to barges and received coal for the local brick industry and shipped its finished products outwards. Coupled with the livestock farming on local agricultural land and the consequent need to get fattened animals to market, this busy area clearly needed a more reliable local means of crossing the river than that offered by the causeway where the depth of water varied and could be dangerously deceptive.

Once known as the King's Ferry, this Combwich river crossing may have dated back to Saxon times but, in addition to the fourteenth century mention, it certainly featured in a will dated 1650 and again in an indenture of 1751. The latter referred to the sale of fifteen acres of land, an orchard, a wharf for landing coal and 'the ferry or passage boat' and 'its customs, profits and privileges'. The crossing was recorded as providing 'large ferry boats for cattle, sheep and passengers in the eighteenth century.'

Today, the eastern approach to the River Parrett opposite Combwich is just a lonely track and the old White House Inn just a ruin along it. It is easier to imagine the days of the ferry in the village setting of the Combwich side, where passengers would wait for the ferry in the Blue Anchor Inn or ring the bell to summon the ferryman from the other side. Less easy to imagine, unless you were out on the riverbank alone on a wild night and with darkness approaching, is the reputed ghostly re-enactment of that evening in the eighteenth century when the horses pulling a coach across the Combwich Passage were startled and bolted, taking the vehicle and its innocent passengers to a watery oblivion.

ANCIENT AXBRIDGE

Axbridge is one of those rare and very special places where the evidence of the past is dramatically apparent, and provides a vivid idea of how a small town would have looked over a long history stretching back to Roman times. Although the name Axbridge has had a variety of spellings over the years there can be little doubt that it can be taken literally and refer to a bridge over the River Axe. That watercourse is now a mile or so away, but has had a host of routes and tributaries over the ages and there is at least one strong view that the original bridge lies buried beneath The Square, which is the heart of the present settlement.

These two fine jettied buildings at the entry to The Square at Axbridge create a vivid idea of what the town would have looked like 500 years ago.

From the town's market square, where the market cross and stocks once stood, the outlook in all direction holds a wealth of special features. The misleadingly misnamed King John's Hunting Lodge commands instant attention, clearly revealing its origins as a late medieval wool merchant's house dating from around 1500 – nearly 300 years after King John's death. At the lower corner of the High Street, dramatically timbered and jettied, it rises three stories from a stone foundation: the ground floor once having been occupied by shops, the second devoted to the living area and workshops and the third to the sleeping and ancillary accommodation.

Now owned by the National Trust and functioning as a museum with local support, the building has been restored to reveal the incredible main timbers around which the construction centres as well as showing the pattern of secondary beams projecting outwards to carry the jetties. Helped by the fact that neither stairs, walls, nor anything else, is really straight inside, and by the collection of artefacts the building houses, it is easy to get some idea of how the original occupants might have lived.

This fine belvedere rises above The Old Courthouse, another of Axbridge's ancient buildings. *(Roy Gallop)*

On the opposite side of the High Street is another timber-framed building of the same period, with a further example at No. 9, a little way along. Further up this narrow, atmospheric street are other period features; huge studded doors, carved lintels and more.

With a little imagination one can visualise the barbaric annual bull-baiting ritual which took place along here every November, and during which the unhappy beast was hounded to its death by a host of local people, supposedly in the interests of tenderising the meat it was then slaughtered to provide.

Moorland Street, leading south, was the route which linked the market area of the Saxon 'burh' of Axbridge to the royal palace at Cheddar. There is a whole host of buildings here from the late fifteenth and early sixteenth century, such as The Old Almshouse. Further along is the former headquarters of the police force for the old Axbridge Division, where a superintendent managed a team of six sergeants and twenty-two constables. The Division used to comprise over forty parishes, and the Axbridge Union workhouse could house some 500 inmates taken from these. Today, the workhouse building survives as modern apartments with pleasant garden surroundings, having had an interim period as a hospital.

At one time, Axbridge even had a mint; its first charter was granted in 1557 and it was an extremely prosperous place at the height of the wool trade, deriving great wealth from the fairs and markets held regularly in the town. These also made a contribution to the ongoing building of the magnificent St John's Church which presides graciously over the town from its elevated position off the market square.

A special corner of Axbridge, not only for churchgoers, but because charity used to be distributed here and the two wells in the retaining wall formed the town's main water supply.

Beside the approach steps are twin wells, fed by water off the Mendip Hillss via a former mill pond. They represent a rare survival of a public water supply with a 500-year history.

Other unusual and intriguing sights around the heart of Axbridge include its charming little 1830s town hall, the Lamb Inn where the Guildhall used to stand and a building with a two-storey frontage but only one storey behind. Despite their aged appearance, quite a few of the buildings in the heart of Axbridge are even older than their frontages and most have a deserved place in the wealth of unusual features with which Axbridge is blessed. A candidate for favourite among them would be The Old Angel, an attractive dwelling with a 500-year history, including one period when it had an alehouse on the ground floor, a gaming room on the first and a parlour above (where morality was not an obvious virtue).

B

BACK-SWORDS AND BROKEN HEADS

The age-old human leaning towards peculiar combinations of skill and aggression that masqueraded under the general heading of games was very evident in Somerset in the eighteenth and nineteenth centuries. One of the favourite pastimes in the county was back-swords, which in essence, consisted of using a mock wooden 'sword' to strike an opponent's head sufficiently hard to make it bleed. Large crowds watched the contests not only as a local attraction at such places as Wincanton, Wiveliscombe, Worle and Wedmore, but also in the form of regular inter-county matches and even a Somerset v. England fixture. Wedmore, in particular, was quite famous for its back-sword players at one period and they travelled far and wide to compete, making a substantial profit for themselves and their backers out of their success.

The basic rule in back-sword contests was that the player to first draw blood from his opponent was the winner, but each engagement followed a prescribed pattern. The two opponents were supported by three seconds, known as 'sticklers', who would help their principal remove his jacket, carry his weapon and generally urge his fearsome reputation upon anyone prepared to listen. Before setting about one another, the contestants would shake hands and voice the wish, 'God save our eyes'. Upon a given signal, the 'swordsmen' would then weave, feint and seek an opportunity for the telling blow, using body strikes to distract the adversary from the real thrust designed to avoid the arm he was using to protect his head. In some contests this elementary defence was replaced with a strap stretched between leg and hand which could be raised to deflect blows. Even so, bruising would have occurred in every contest, possibly as the least painful outcome, and sometimes the rivalry might get totally out of hand and an onlooker free-for-all ensue.

At irregular intervals over the years, Somerset men took on those of Berkshire and Wiltshire at a back-sword event known as 'The Scouring of the White Horse'. John Bunn of Wedmore was the champion at the Scouring event in 1857, but not all the contests went the county's way. When they did, a common rumour (no doubt started by disappointed contestants or punters) was that Somerset men did not bleed so readily as others as they drank cider and vinegar before a match to inhibit the flow of blood. Whatever the outcome, those taking part would do

(From a Thomas Bewick woodcut)

quite well out of the occasion, for after each bout they would walk round and collect offerings from the spectators in the wicker hand guard of their weapon.

A variant of back-swords was 'sword and dagger', where the principal weapon was a 2ft long stout stick, with a striking knob at one end and a wicker hand guard at the other. This game was one of the main features of a two-day event held at Langport in 1768, when a purse of two guineas was offered for the contestant who 'broke the most heads' on the first day and one guinea for the winner of each of the sword and dagger and back-swords contests on the second. The White Horse Inn provided a meal on both days to sustain the spectators, who could also watch the various other opportunities to see blood spilled by contestants or animals. In Somerton the venue for such events was the Red Lion, where a customary prize was a gold-laced hat.

Wood also replaced the metal of earlier times, in other events that featured regularly on feast, fair and other special occasions. The quarter staff had been about and used in contests for centuries.

The normal length was 5 or 6ft and the standard practice was to hold the staff in the centre with one hand and move the other to create the variety of swings and strikes. There was also a version of back-swords in which the contestants each stood in a barrel, ducking down to avoid blows and popping up again in the hope of catching their opponent off guard.

Cudgel contests in their formal mode were much the same as back-sword play. Rather different was the local pastime of throwing a cudgel, or any suitable stout piece of wood for that matter, as far or as high as could be achieved. Some local contests involved throwing the cudgel over the church, with the champion open to a return match challenge or one from a neighbouring village. Cudgel events were a regular feature of life in places as far apart as Dundry, Wiveliscombe and Wincanton.

BATH BRICKS

Where 'Bath Bricks' got their name is a mystery. They don't come from Bath, their use is not confined to the bath or baths and they were not discovered by a Mr Bath. Be that as it may, these scouring blocks were a major Somerset industry for around 100 years. At its height this important industry, largely based in Bridgwater, was selling millions of tons of its product annually. It was in use in every corner of the British Empire, Europe and the New World, and it was a staple wherever regular cleaning took place, from public baths to hospital sluices and army barracks to warship decks. A powdered brick kept metal objects clean, and if dampened with water, it was highly effective on floors and similar large surfaces.

The bricks themselves were about the size of a double bar of the old square soap blocks and were composed largely of gritty particles of silica and alumina, with lime, sulphur and clay in smaller amounts. The natural flow of the River Parrett brought these materials downriver towards Bridgwater, where they encountered other deposits moving up river with the tides and were deposited in the best proportions for their ultimate purpose in a short stretch of the river either side of the town bridge.

Between Somerset Bridge to the south and the town bridge itself, Bath brick works existed on both sides of the river, but further down they were mainly on the eastern bank.

The deposited mixture which constituted the raw material for Bath bricks was known as 'slime', for it was an unattractive dirty colour, and the areas of its collection were referred to as 'batches'. A seeming bonanza for Bridgwater; but the process conflicted with the desire of the shipping interests to keep the

The slime batches for collecting the raw materials for Bath bricks stretched for about 2 miles in either direction from the Bridgwater's Town Bridge.

river as deep and free as possible, while the Bath brick manufacturers offered some strong opposition to the eroder boats built for that purpose.

The potential for this special Bridgwater slime seems to have been increasingly realised from around 1820 and, at its peak, bricks were being manufactured at the rate of over 20 million tons a year, the bulk of them being exported by sea from the Bridgwater wharves. The major manufacturers of conventional bricks and tiles found it a lucrative supplementary activity which fitted in well with their core business. Between the two World Wars more sophisticated products appeared and gradually displaced the simple Bath brick.

Processing the slime to produce the scouring bricks was a dirty, labour-intensive job. First the base of each batch was laid down, preferably where the river had a slight inward curve and thus a slower current to encourage the deposit process. Rubble from the adjacent brickyards was used as a bed and a slight sill was provided to contain the settling process. When the deposit had reached 4ft or so, it was dug out manually and left on the riverbank for rain to wash out the unwanted salt content. Next, when the weather was better, it went into a horse-worked mixer – the 'pugging mill' – for women and boys to gather the output into balls containing the amount needed to fill a mould. Thus 'obstricked', the balled mixture was pressed into the mould using a 'striker' to achieve its final brick shape. The shaped bricks then stood on drying boards for a few days.

WHITBYS' BRIDGWATER ALMANACK AND TIDE TABLE.

Bridgwater Bath . . . Bricks. . .

The Original and Genuine Bath or Scouring Bricks can now be obtained in Cargoes, Truck Loads, and carefully packed in Boxes for Export, direct from the MANUFACTURERS,

Messrs. HUNT & ROBINS,
BRIDGWATER.

PRICES ON APPLICATION. Telegrams and Cables: HUNT, BRIDGWATER.

After drying, the shaped mixture was fired in high temperature kilns. After it had cooled, each brick got a surface trim with an emery wheel; any misshapen ones being powdered for sale in that form. The bricks then got a wrapper of strong paper and were boxed or crated for shipment or home disposal. Bridgwater's own sailing vessels, plus others bringing in coal and other cargoes to the port, found regular employment in carrying the Bath brick exports, along with the movement of conventional bricks and tiles. Some of the smaller vessels, as well as local barges, also helped to bring slime from the more distant batches to the main processing areas.

Bridgwater received a major contribution to its prosperity from this near-unique business. Bath bricks are now just a memory, but in their day they prompted praise like that in one advertisement which boldly stated: 'Bath brick will be found to be the most effective and economical polishing material. It is superior to metal polish and does not contain acid or alcohol injurious to metals.'

BEFORE BEAU NASH

The mineral waters of Bath have been important since the misty times of the legendary leper Prince Bladud, who was cast out from his people until he found a cure. His pigs had been bathing in a warm swamp and discovered a remedy for their various ailments. Upon trying it himself, Badud realised that he too was cured. Today, Bath has a modern spa facility and atmospheric Pump Room, which are popular successors to a former heyday, when Beau Nash dictated fashion and behaviour and the well-to-do 'took' the waters and enjoyed an indulgent pattern of social entertainment. Centuries earlier, the Romans had taken full advantage of the natural springs and created a complex of baths and heated rooms as part of a temple to Sulis Minerva. The Saxon nobility continued the bathing habit, but from the Norman Conquest onwards the story of Bath's curative waters is anything but straightforward and at times was extremely unsavoury.

The very existence of Bath, or Aquae Sulis as the Romans named it, is linked to its three springs, in which water rises to the surface after having been heated and forced upwards by the higher temperatures deep below the earth's crust. After their subterranean journey, these waters were used to feed the Hot Bath, the Cross Bath and the Kings and Queens Baths, the latter pair forming the core of the Pump Room complex.

Over the centuries their warmth and multi-mineral content have proved beneficial to countless visitors, who have cleansed their systems by drinking the water, or eased their skin and muscular complaints by bathing in it. In addition to their soothing warmth, the Bath waters contained over forty minerals and, in former years when too much lead was used in food, drink and other items, drinking it in quantity was often highly beneficial, even if only by diluting the lead intake.

The imposing entrance to the Pump Room complex, with the Kings and Queens Baths beyond.

Bath had to be rebuilt after suffering in post-Conquest quarrels between William's two sons, but John de Villula, an adventurer whose enterprise brought him a bishop's appointment, bought Bath from the king for 550 marks and established two new baths there. Later bishops added to the number of hospitals linked to the baths, and the revenues from the latter went to the local monastic orders. This link between the waters and healing continued when a Leper's Bath was added to the hospital dedicated to St Lazarus, possibly as early as 1138, its waters being drawn from the Hot Bath.

For centuries bathing was essentially a local activity, part of the hospitals' care for the sick, and little more than the use of mineral springs for their reputed healing properties. Of the two separate but adjacent baths, the Cross Bath was the larger of the two, but still measured only 25ft at its widest point. Flanked by stone arches and simple dressing rooms, its waters were more temperate than those of its companion, the Hot Bath. This was both the smallest and the hottest of the baths, until it was enlarged to match its neighbour. The water furthest from the main source proved cooler and could be used by those who did not want to be 'parboyled', as one writer put it. Both baths were used by those with skin ailments, although the Hot Bath had a few side baths for the private use of those more fastidious about their bathing companions. These baths were really quite small and open to the elements, apart from a few arches in the surrounding walls which provided a little basic shelter.

The King's Bath, near the abbey, was always the most impressive of the baths with a high wall and separate arches for men and women. In its post-medieval form it had four entrances, referred to as 'slips', leading from the dressing rooms to the water level, itself surrounded by a paved walkway. Many small improvements resulted from the donations of grateful users; additions such as walkway rails and rings for bathers to hold on to. Some 60ft long, the King's Bath was provided with such refinements as a spout facility to concentrate the flow of water, drawn from a reservoir beneath. The water also supplied the adjacent Queen's Bath, which could be accessed by a small door separating the two.

In the early centuries the responsibility for the baths and arrangements for their maintenance and control were often muddled and inept, leading to laxity and unseemly behaviour in their use. Bishop Beckynton was complaining as early as 1449 about the habit of stripping new bathers of their smock or drawers. He roundly declared that anyone who had reached the age of puberty should avoid revealing themselves to bystanders. Matters do not seem to have improved a century later when Doctor Turner recorded in 1562 that 'we make no partition between ye men and the weomen whiles they are in bathing, but suffer them … to go together lyke unreasonable beastes to the destruction of both body and soul of very manye.' Prominent citizen John Wood referred to, 'people of both sexes bathing by day and night naked; and dogs, cats and pigs and even human creatures were hurl'd over the rails into the water.'

Until 1610 the water drunk at the baths had no separate conduits, but the drinking did at least take place before the bathing started. At this time, management of the baths was still very poor, with only erratic cleaning and virtually no control over who bathed and how they conducted themselves. The users were a mixed bag, including local sportsmen from the tennis courts, as well as those partaking in other physical activities. Around the baths, a steady increase in visitors had produced a group of dwellings adapted, often poorly, for their accommodation. They were also intended to house a new breed of attendant physicians, intent as much on profit as on healing. Again, the period was a mixture of good and bad, with one writer describing the latter in very graphic terms:

> A person would … find himself landed in a little, close, unsavoury town, and in the danger of being torn limb from limb by a swarm of harpies in the shape of lodging-house keepers. The apartments in which he was at last installed were not of the kind to revive spirits exhausted by illness and fatigue … The bed furniture was of the coarsest description; the floor was coloured brown by a mixture of soot and small beer, and splashed with droppings from the whitewash which plastered the walls and chimney-pieces. The first care of the landlord, after settling an extortionate rent for himself, would be to introduce the patient (to) his accomplice whose job it was to prove that the bath nearest the lodging in question was the only one in town suited to the patient's complaints.

The rise of merchant guilds and the growth of the cloth trade brought increasing prosperity to Bath, replacing the influence of the monasteries and the loss of some of its religious status to Wells. The sick and crippled still came to benefit from the waters, and more and more physicians took up residence in the city; but it was the visits of Queen Anne (the wife of James I) and the entertainment provided for her that began the trend for something more than the bathing process alone. Helping to fill the gap left by the relocation of the cloth trade, this process resumed after the Civil War, and by the 1660s visitors were arriving from all over the British Isles.

Drinking the mineral waters from the Bath springs became popular, and it was being bottled and sold widely by the seventeenth century. Whatever the benefits, the taste was not a totally pleasant one, judging from one of the many writings that gave advice on how to deal with conditions brought on by the bathing or drinking process. For the latter, one particular piece of advice recommended adding herbs and spices to a pot of water from the King's Bath, then standing it in boiling water overnight and, in the morning, adding white wine, sugar and lemon juice. The same writer also provided remedies for conditions brought on by bathing such as 'marring the stomach' and 'heating of the kidneys or liver.'

The views on Bath that were expressed by various visitors were by no means uniform. Samuel Pepys in 1668 described the city as 'clean' and made no adverse comment on his two bathing experiences. On the first he went to the Cross Bath at 4 a.m. expecting it to be quiet at that early hour, but remarked that it was

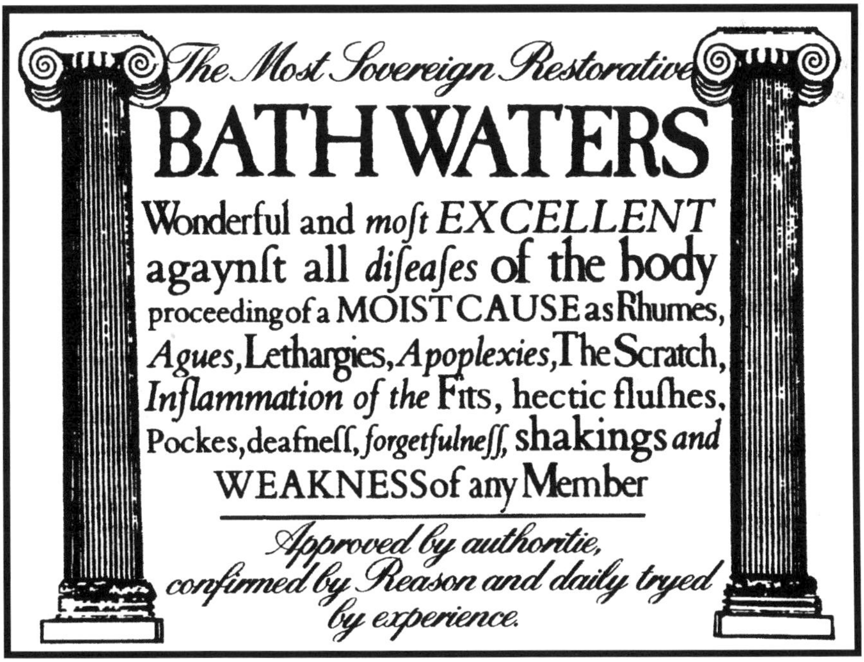

soon quite busy with gentry. After a couple of hours he took a chair back to his lodgings and went to bed for an hour to sweat out the immersion. Then, after a day in Bristol, he was back in the baths again at 10 p.m. A subsequent visit to The King's Bath he found full of more cosmopolitan users.

A writer in 1675 described his own bathing experience in the following words:

> There met we all kinde of Persons, of all Shapes, and Formes, of all Degrees, of all Countreys, and of all Diseases, of both Sexes: for to see the young and old, riche and poore; blind and lame; diseased and sound; Engish and French; men and women; Boyes and Girls, one with another, peepe up in their caps and appeare so markedly and fearfully, in their uncouth naked Postures, would a little astound and put one in mind of the Resurrection.

Prompted by the increasing number of bathers, a series of improvements were made to the baths in 1676, with by-laws to regulate conduct and a supervisory body installed to enforce them. It would seem that these sufficiently achieved their objectives to encourage Queen Mary, the second wife of James II, to make a visit in 1687, hoping to end her infertility; she found that the Cross Bath did the trick. In the eighteenth century, the baths moved into a new and more wholesome era.

BEWITCHED

A young Harptree woman with the surname Griffin lost her father and mother quite early in her life. The father had been a successful farmer and left his daughter quite well off, so that with a kindly aunt and uncle to take care of her, the young lady managed to come to terms with the tragedy and get on with her life, enjoying a reasonable degree of comfort and happiness. Until, that is, the day that Dame Fowler came knocking at her door.

Miss Griffin was alone at the time, and on the pretext of wanting to sell her some matches, her elderly caller managed to insinuate herself into the house and persuade the young woman to have her fortune told. With the cards laid out in front of her, the old lady painted a lurid and detailed picture of what life held in store for Miss Griffin and then demanded 5*s* for doing so. A refusal to pay this exorbitant sum resulted in a series of wild threats, and although she accepted a shilling and some food, it was clear that Dame Fowler was less than happy with the transaction. She left the house grumbling and assuring Miss Griffin that she would have cause to regret her unwillingness to pay up.

Within a week, the once healthy and happy maiden had become a different person, pale, worried and with no appetite at all. This state of affairs continued, with her torment of the nights being even worse than the anxieties of the day. As the recorder of Miss Griffin's tribulations put it, 'for some time she had nightly been awakened by some monster of hideous form, pressing on her body with such force that she could scarcely breathe, which lasted three, and sometimes four, hours.'

Eventually, the tormented girl told her aunt and uncle about her unwelcome caller and of the dreadful nightly visits from the 'monster of hideous form' and the terrifying experience which ensued. Try as the older folk might, they could not shake their niece out of her unhappy state.

Matters got steadily worse until the uncle, in desperation, suggested that poor Miss Griffin should 'take a long sharp awl blade to bed with her, and plunge it into the monster.' By now willing to grasp at any possible way of ending her ordeal, the young woman took his advice that very same night. When the monster appeared and loomed darkly over her, the distraught girl plunged the blade into its form with all her might, so fiercely that it snapped off. With a wild cry the dreadful figure vanished.

But the matter did not end there. The next morning the village was buzzing with the rumour that old Dame Fowler 'had runned a spike into her side' and was badly hurt. Miss Griffin dashed over to the old woman's house to see if the talk was correct and found that a local healer skilled in herbs and potions had treated the injured lady and removed the spike from her body. It 'exactly matched' the weapon Miss Griffin had used the night before!

The chronicler of these events now refers to Dame Fowler as a witch and ends his account by recording that the 'old hag was apprehended, and fully committed to the House of Correction till the Assizes, when she will take her trial for Witchcraft.'

BIRD IN THE HAND

In rural counties like Somerset, the economic survival of many ordinary families depended greatly on wives and children adding their labour to that of the main breadwinner. According to one account derived from church records, 'nearly everybody in the parish seems to have added to his income by slaying pole-cats, stoats, hedgehogs, sparrows, joys (jays), and pie-magobs (magpies), and laying them at the churchwarden's feet.' Behind this activity lies the down-to-earth requirement to keep crops and livestock free of predators and preserve the church's tithe income, plus the useful addition that wild creatures might make to the family diet.

At the very least, the additional labour available within a family would involve cultivating a garden plot and caring for the animals while, at the other end of the scale, hundreds of women had a near-full time job as an outworker for the gloving and shoe industries, to list just two examples. Even more wives and children were expected to put aside everything else and provide extra hands for the harvest periods.

The traditional willow industry of West Sedgemoor, for example, was highly dependent on seasonal help. Wives of willow smallholders would weed, cut and strip the crop on their own or rented land, while on the bigger plots women worked with the men during the autumn cutting peak. Older children joined in the April and May task of stripping the willows after winter storage, either after school or instead of it. In the nineteenth century, the normal payment was sixpence per stripped bundle, often paid in local tokens.

Protecting all crops against natural predators was a national issue which was seen as vitally important. As early as 1532, legislation required each parish to provide nets for trapping birds. For the next 300 years various churchwardens' accounts recorded payments to those trapping and killing with 'prices' ranging from a halfpenny a head for bullfinches (Minehead) to twopence each for kites (Porlock). The prices for birds like sparrows remained surprisingly stable, but by 1837 Martock was paying out for 5,988 of them!

Wild animals were another prime target and source of extra earnings. Skilful use of dogs, traps and lures could result in vestry payments for hedgehogs, badgers, foxes and otters (Cheddar). Polecats, often known as firchets or feeches, also appeared in the records, but the twopence they fetched seems a bit low for the effort that would have been involved in finding and trapping this elusive animal.

(From a Thomas Bewick woodcut)

It all seems very cruel by today's standards and most of the vermin statutes were repealed in 1863. Well before that, the Minehead vestry had resolved not to pay out any more parish money for killing 'any foxes, badgers or other vemint or destructive birds.' With the commutation of tithes, the church had less interest in the matter and local families had to earn their extra income direct from the landowners.

BODYSNATCHERS AT WORK

The expression 'worth more dead than alive' may possibly refer to the macabre nineteenth-century crime of bodysnatching, which even occurred in Somerset. The dissection of dead bodies was legalised in the time of Henry VIII, and for a long time the demands of medical science were met by the instrument of the gallows. A specific or implicit feature of the death sentence was that the corpse of a convicted felon should be given to a teaching hospital or anatomical school. For centuries, harsh laws and judgements meant that the supply of bodies kept pace with demand, but with no regulation of these establishments until the Anatomy Act of 1832, that balance began to change as their numbers, fuelled by the appetite for greater medical knowledge, increased.

(From a Thomas Bewick woodcut)

By the early years of the nineteenth century a shortage of subjects for dissection led to an increase in the unsavoury crime of bodysnatching, and a shady trade in trafficking the newly deceased. Although the demand came from London and other large cities, there were no distinctions about the source of supply, and Somerset was not immune from the nocturnal activities of bodysnatchers. The going rate was between £12 10*s* and £15 a corpse, a sum that proved a great temptation to thieves.

The Bridgwater area featured in some disturbing examples of bodysnatching which came to light in 1829. Shortly after New Year, a Mrs Watkins of Silver Street died and was duly buried at Durleigh. Suspicions which arose soon afterwards led to the opening of the grave, and the discovery that her body had been stolen. As the news got around, a smell was noticed coming from a basket left at the coach office of the Castle & Falcon for despatch on the London stagecoach. It was opened and inside was found not the missing Mrs Watkins, but the remains of a very young boy.

There was an immediate investigation which revealed that several other bodies had been stolen from local graveyards. One incident came to light when another basket, brought in to the George for despatch to a London address, was being moved. Through a gap in the wickerwork an astonished porter found his fingers touching a human foot. It proved to belong to a lady who had died in childbirth and been buried at Cannington. The sender of the basket was never traced.

Some churches erected a watch house in order to guard against this form of desecration. Others had heavy stone slabs that could be placed on a grave, left there for several weeks and then be re-used elsewhere once the corpse had lost its freshness and thus its value. Long Ashton had a large ledger stone and used it on graves to foil intending robbers from nearby Bristol. A similar method at Huntspill, where the stone still exists, formed part of a sad but romantic story.

It is said that a Miss Rogers of Huntspill Court died of a broken heart after news that her sailor fiancé had drowned on his way home for their wedding. On her deathbed she had expressed a wish to be buried in her wedding gown and adorned with her best jewellery. This might have been too much of a temptation for potential grave robbers, so a heavy stone was laid on top of the poor lady's grave and a watch kept there until the danger was considered to be over.

Among the other measures to combat this macabre trend was the use of iron coffins, the first design being patented in 1818. They were not popular with the clergy, as the iron vessel would not decompose and thus prevented the reuse of the site. After the 1832 legislation, the bodysnatching problem largely disappeared as a result of a provision that dead bodies could be sold for dissection if not claimed within seventy-two hours of death. The graves of Somerset could finally enjoy the peace to which they were entitled.

BRUNEL'S BERTHA

Bertha was not an official name, but it was the one by which a unique vessel was known to all who had anything to do with the docks at Bridgwater. Although her purpose there was the same as that of a dredger, she was not one in the technical sense, being more properly a drag boat that acted rather like a waterborne bulldozer, but with her scraper blade at the rear.

Brunel had devised this concept at Bristol, which prompted the building of a vessel to put it into practice in the clearance of mud in Bristol's Floating Harbour. Known simply as *BD6*, she was built in Bristol by Bush & Beddoe and cost the dock company £749, continuing at work there until the 1960s. The idea was adopted for solving similar silting problems at Bridgwater after the Bridgwater & Taunton Canal had been extended to a new dock, linking it with the River Parrett on the northern side of the town in 1841. Very soon it was found that tidal mud from the river was entering the new dock with incoming vessels and reducing the depth of water available for shipping. On the recommendation of the eminent canal and dock engineer William Cubitt, it was decided to order a similar machine to Bristol's *BD6*.

Also built in Bristol, this second drag boat arrived in Bridgwater in time to start work in 1844. She was a 60 ton ugly duckling of a vessel approximately 50ft long, 14ft wide, and resembling an elongated shoe box with flat bows and stern sloping inwards to the water. From the latter a metal scraper blade was lowered by chain, attached to a guide pole which stuck up in the air even higher than the tall chimney. The riveted puddle iron plates of her hull arrived by ship from Bristol and were assembled at the dock. She was given a plain wooden superstructure with simple covers for the machinery and a simple shelter for the operator, plus a winch and other bits and pieces. *Bertha* had no pretensions when it came to appearance.

The entirely functional drag boat *Bertha* lies unmanned and unused in Bridgwater dock after its closure, awaiting decisions that will eventually secure her survival and preservation.

For power *Bertha* was fitted with a single-cylinder, double-acting steam engine with an upright boiler providing steam at 40psi. A reduction spur wheel drive led to a cross-mounted shaft carrying a flywheel, a chain drum and a winch. The vessel was not self-propelled, but instead pulled itself across the dock by winding in a heavy chain secured on dockside bollards. With the scraper blade lowered, this allowed *Bertha* to move excess mud to a suitable spot for subsequent flushing out. She could then winch in a lighter chain, with the scraper raised, to return to the other side of the dock and repeat the motion. By moving the heavy chain along to the next adjoining bollard at the end of each sweep, the whole dock could be cleared.

The original operation involved collecting the offending mud in the inner dock basin in this way, followed by further complicated manoeuvres to move it into the outer tidal basin where sluices washed it out into the main river. The dock silting problem was never quite solved; dockside cranes and a conventional dredger were tried, but matters did improve when the Great Western Railway laid a culvert of cast iron pipes under the floor of the tidal basin to improve the process of washing out the slime.

Although the owners, British Railways, offered the docks to the Borough of Bridgwater in 1965 they had come to the end of their conventional working life and were subsequently closed. *Bertha* passed to the Exeter Maritime Museum and, more recently, to Eyemouth for restoration work, a fitting tribute to what is possibly the oldest working steam vessel in the world.

C

CANAL CALAMITIES

It seemed a good idea at the time, but a group of Glastonbury entrepreneurs came to regret being swept along by the tide of change, and in particular of canal building, which began in the years around the end of the eighteenth century. Their enterprise, barely remembered or marked today, encountered a host of setbacks and eventually came to the ignominious end of being used to create the fabric of its victorious railway rival.

To replace the former wool and silk businesses which had sustained Glastonbury for many years, a group of influential citizens, led by their young town clerk Richard Perriam Prat, decided to call a public meeting to lobby support for a canal from the town to Highbridge. It was to bring coal, timber and bricks into the area and take agricultural produce to wider markets, and make both canal owners and local tradespeople rich in the process. The year of these meetings, 1825, was also significant for the opening of the pioneering Stockton & Darlington Railway, but only the most far-sighted could foresee that canals would eventually be exposed to the fierce and fatal competition of this new means of transport.

The first survey for the proposed new canal was carried out by a local man, Richard Hammett of Street. He had constructed a few short artificial waterways and hit upon the right route for this larger venture, but his estimate of construction

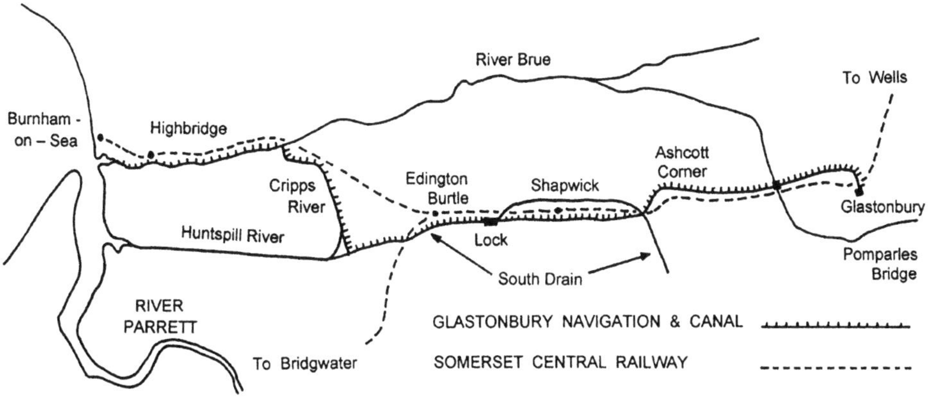

costs was hopelessly low and created a false optimism among the canal's advocates. Hammett's recommendations involved a floating basin at Highbridge, the use of the River Brue to Cripp's Corner, a new cut from there to the South Drain and a final section into Glastonbury via Cuckoo Ditch and the Mill Stream.

The necessary works could be done for less than £10,000, Hammett reckoned; this assumption, together with a prospective return on capital of 10 per cent, appeared in the company's prospectus.

Doubts soon arose about the initial survey and its costings, and a second report by another local man, John Beauchamp, came up with a more realistic estimate of £15,234 for the construction costs. Despite this rise, the need for improved transport access to Glastonbury and the benefit a canal could give in relieving the age-old winter flooding problems of the area kept the promoters optimistic. With £14,000 promised and the main land consents obtained they made their application to Parliament and secured the Royal Assent for their Glastonbury Navigation & Canal Bill in 1827.

So far, so good, but this had been the easy part. As the work on construction got under way, weaknesses began to appear in the assumptions of both earlier surveys. The proprietors had no alternative but to reassess the matter again and engaged the canal engineer John Rennie to undertake the review task. He offered three options, ranging from a waterway for small barges to one for large seagoing vessels. A middle option of catering for large barges and small coastal vessels was chosen, but even this was likely to cost £27,720; nearly three times the original Hammett figure.

Construction of the Glastonbury Canal took from 1829 to 1833 – four years filled with a mixture of progress and problems. Agricultural depression locally meant that the money was slow to come in. The Commissioners of Sewers demanded a £1,000 surety that the clauses in the Act which protected their interests would be observed. At the end of December 1830, the contractor at the Highbridge end was found to be excavating on the wrong side of the turnpike road. By the following February he had 'run away' and the work was at a standstill. Some of the puddling work at the other end would also prove substandard at a later date.

Despite all the setbacks the Glastonbury Canal opened on 15 August 1833, thanks to assistance from the Exchequer Bill Loan Commission. Although the total cost had risen to around £30,000, the event was accompanied by a great celebration. The canal company's barge *Goodland* led a flotilla of craft along the canal to Highbridge, accompanied by cheering crowds on the canal banks and a boat-load of musicians filling the air with stirring music. Church bells rang and musket and cannon were fired. Eleven days later a second celebration was laid on for 'members of the respectable trading class', but one of the boats used, the new yacht *St Vincent* sprang a leak and was in real danger of sinking. Fortunately the *Goodland* was able to effect a rescue, but the Glastonbury Canal had witnessed another bad omen.

The remains of the lock where the former Glastonbury Canal began, via the original course of the River Brue at Highbridge.

Such records as exist suggest that the new canal did carry a fair amount of traffic in the next few years, but far less than the proprietors had hoped for, partly due to the fact that every time the cost estimates had risen the forecast of prospective business had been optimistically increased to keep the scheme viable.

Soon the consequences of false economies began to emerge; the first was at Edington Burtle, where mistakes and corner-cutting by the contractors had resulted in places with no bottoming work and weaknesses in the bank lining. Combined with the weight of excavated material along the banks, the peat underlying the canal became waterlogged and forced the bottom upwards, resulting in a serious reduction in the water depth. Larger vessels could no longer use the upper section and attempts to admit more water from the River Brue just led to complaints from local farmers. At the Highbridge end there was insufficient water to sluice out the silt in the lock area.

The outlook for the Glastonbury Canal was dismal. Traffic was sparse and the implications of the forthcoming railway intrusion were now obvious in the work taking place on the route of the infant Bristol & Exeter Railway. In January 1840 the canal's solicitor and leading supporter absconded owing some £50,000, this being attributed 'to the unprosperous state of the Glastonbury Canal.' Another major figure leapt to his death from the high tower of St John's Church.

The canal enterprise managed to struggle on for a while, but traffic only amounted to a few barge loads a week. Finally, in 1847, a deal was done with the Bristol & Exeter Railway, which acquired the navigation for just £7,372. The new owners had their own round of disputes over water levels with the Commissioners of Sewers, but then sold the canal on to Somerset Central Railway, which embodied much of the canal route in the line it opened from Highbridge to Glastonbury on 17 August 1854. Three years earlier, one of the new railway's promoters had recorded, 'I spent all day at Glastonbury winding up the affairs of the canal and distributing the wreck of its fortune among the shareholders.'

CAVE DWELLER

Most highwaymen used inns as their source of information about travellers likely to prove good pickings. Many also used the more remote taverns as their permanent base and often lived there, secure in a warning system they had arranged with the landlord. However, a highwayman named Pocock is said to have had somewhat different arrangements for his personal accommodation. He lived in a cave.

The location of Pocock's hideout was on the wooded hillside near Chilton Polden village and close to the priory. It was well chosen; the road along the top of the hill between Bridgwater and Glastonbury had been well-used since Roman times and this was the route that coaches from Bridgwater and beyond took for their journeys to and from London. For highwaymen and footpads it offered excellent prospects of ill-gotten gains. Furthermore, although the Polden hills average little more than 200ft in height, this was still enough to reveal both potential victims, and also possible threats.

Pocock's home was rather more than just a hole in the hillside. As caves go, it was a three-room luxury apartment. The outer 'room' was for the highwayman's horse, no doubt because it gave the most headroom and would be handy if a quick getaway was needed. Next came the living room and beyond it a smaller room for sleeping in. This cave location was not only convenient and snug, but Pocock was protected by the high regard held for him locally, which he nurtured by giving away some of the money he stole. Not only that but, on principle, he never robbed a woman or child and was said to be helpful to any deserving or stranded traveller. Apocryphal maybe, but it was also thought that Pocock's horse had specially designed shoes which helped it to veer sharply away from pursuing riders!

Despite his 'Robin Hood' reputation, Pocock's cave was eventually discovered by the authorities. Although he fought a bloody battle, the robber himself was taken and hauled off to an end on the gallows. The cave that had been his home and banditry headquarters was eventually sealed off when some of the props supporting the roof gave way and the entrance was closed forever.

So ended this somewhat different man and his unusual lair, but for many years Pocock was remembered locally in a rhyme:

Rynne, mye boyes, ryne, the moon shines bryte,
Pocock's yn hys cave, his pyrsse is lyte;
But, whenne the nighte ys myrke ande darke,
Hee's offe wyth hys steede, blythe as a larke.

CLEEVE CORRODIANS

A corrodian was a person who paid to be accommodated, usually in a monastery, in old age. A lump sum would be paid in advance, and the facilities were duly provided. Such arrangements represented another source of income for an abbey or monastery to add to the rents, bequests, market tolls and other monies coming in, which in turn were spent on the upkeep of the establishment, support of the monks and on the religious and charitable works it carried out.

Pre-Dissolution religious foundations were generally housed in large and impressive buildings to glorify God and facilitate their many functions. There was frequently sufficient room not only to cater for brothers too old for normal life, but also enough spare accommodation for other worthy and wealthy candidates who wanted to be provided for in their old age. The latter might include the senior retainers of a person of high influence and, in the case of Muchelney Abbey, it actually included former officers of the royal court.

Cleeve Abbey was neither a large nor a rich establishment, being classed as small in the examinations which took place prior to the Dissolution. It had been set up on a grant of land around the beginning of the thirteenth century, and in line with the practices of the Cistercian order, was a somewhat spartan place internally, where its white-robed brothers spent long hours in work and prayer. It was often in debt, and the income from corrodians represented a welcome addition to the budget.

The two corrodian 'suites' at Cleeve were occupied in the abbey's later years by Margaret Johnson and John Michel. The former had probably worked in or for the abbey prior to retirement, for she continued to make a contribution by providing spices for use in the guest house, and was paid for this service. Her corrodian arrangement included the weekly provision of seven loaves, twelve pounds of candles and five gallons of ale. John Michel received seven dishes of fish or meat in addition to his loaves and ale and both were supplied with periodical loads of wood.

The gateway of Cleeve Abbey, still impressive after years of decay, but clearly needing the care it now receives from English Heritage.

The corrodian accommodation was among the abbey's south side buildings, furthest from the abbey church but, sensibly, adjacent to the refectory and warming room. The £27 paid by Edward Walker gave him a personal suite of two high-ceilinged, decorated rooms for use as sitting room and bedroom plus a lavatory, and separate accommodation was provided for servants and horses. He could eat with the abbot if he wished, but he had his own fireplace and oven and a supply of wood for fuel.

Despite Cleeve Abbey's reputation for 'priests of honest life' and for its extensive hospitality and charity, it could not escape the process of Dissolution and duly succumbed in 1537, when its religious community and pensioner guests would have been faced with upheaval and relocation.

COCK AND BULL

The fashionable enjoyment of such cruel sports as cockfighting and bull baiting was led by the moneyed classes who could afford extravagant diversions and constantly sought new ones, with few reservations about expense or censure. Indeed, both the Elizabeth I and James I are known to have enjoyed watching the baiting of bulls and bears, while Henry VIII had built a magnificent octagonal cockpit at his Whitehall palace, with tiered seats for the spectators and a special viewing place for himself as part of the cock cage. The Church did not share these enthusiasms as it distracted people from worship, and a few other voices warned of the social consequences, one expressing the belief that cockfighting 'has trained many a victim for the gallows and reduced many a family to want and begging.'

Bull baiting enjoyed an element of respectability as it was seen as an essential way of tenderising the meat of the animal. Several towns in Somerset had ordinances actually requiring the harrying of bulls by dogs and at Wells in 1608, for example, a number of butchers were indicted because they had offered meat which had not been 'pulsatus' (baited to tenderise it). Less justifiable was the annual Axbridge practice involving the mob beating a bull to death with clubs and then handing the carcass over to the cagman to cut it up for the benefit of the poor. At Burnham-on-Sea as late as the 1920s there was a bullfight of the Spanish kind in a great tent filled with paying spectators.

Birds were generally considered as crop predators, and a source of food which justified their slaughter somewhat. Infinitely more reprehensible was the vicious use of gamecocks in cockfighting, where the main objectives were to satisfy a desire for betting and a sad relish in bloody conflict. As much attention was focused on the breeding, training and matching of these cocks as would today only be enjoyed by champion dogs or horses.

Matching gamecocks was widespread in cockpits all over Somerset prior to the nineteenth century when it became illegal nationally by virtue of the Cruelty of Animals Act of 1849. After that, cockpit owners faced a fine of £5 a day if caught and might even go to prison. In the previous century, however, the 'sport' had achieved a considerable status, with well-organised prestige contests taking place between groups of bird owners both within Somerset and with neighbouring counties. Most took place in the summer months; Shrove Tuesday in particular was associated with cock fights.

One of the venues for the traditional Somerset v. Dorset battles was the Red Lion Inn at Somerton. A *Western Flying Post* advertisement in 1761 gave notice of one such event which, it stated, would:

> Show Thirty-One Main Cocks each Side, for Four Guineas a Battle, and Forty Guineas the Odd Battle; to weigh on Tuesday the 12th May, and to fight the two following days. Each Gentleman to feed his own Cocks.

At Hinton Charterhouse three years earlier there had been a 'Battle Royal' with a special prize of a gold-laced hat and a proviso that the landlord involved was entitled to retain all the dead cocks. Sometimes the bird feeders were specified to ensure their impartial status, and an event might well be preceded by an afternoon meal. It was a social occasion as well as a spectacle and a prime opportunity to make or lose money.

At one time this house in Somerton was the *New Inn* and a writer in 1935 refers to having seen the remains of a cockpit in the attic there.

A two-day session of cockfighting at the Castle Tavern at Taunton was advertised as an 'amicable meeting', but the inter-county contests like the annual Shrove Tuesday event at Ansford were quite formal affairs. This was to be expected, in view of the amount of effort invested in breeding, feeding, grooming and preparing the gamecocks and the often considerable sums of money wagered on their performance. Complex rules existed governing the handling of the birds, addressing such as issues as when to 'set to', how to deal with an injured bird and what constituted a refusal and the call of 'no battle'. The Master of the Match, or Cock Master, was firmly in charge, and there were strict conduct rules, including a provision that anyone defaulting on a bet might be put in a basket suspended in the cockpit so that all present should be aware of his shame! The Master might also require a minor official to vacate a prime seat in the lower ring to 'make room for those of the better sort'!

Matches in the countless local cockpits were less formal, but all the contests had in common the degrading spectacle of birds inflicting terrible damage on one another. Even the survivors lost most of their feathers, suffered deep and painful wounds and might even lose an eye, especially if the contest rules permitted the birds to be fitted with spurs.

Cocks were also the unlucky victims in several other so-called sports. One of these was 'Cock Squailing', described as 'a barbarous game, consisting of tying a cock to a stake, and throwing a stick at him from a given distance, so as to destroy the bird.' The cock was normally tethered by one leg, and a small fee was charged for the right to throw. In one version, a thrower knocking the cock down could keep him if he got to the spot before the bird recovered. In another, the cock was suspended in a pot and won by the thrower who could break it. When this sort of cruelty was made illegal, model cocks of clay or other materials were used, the Bleadon one being made of a cabbage stalk decorated with red flannel and feathers. Smaller model cocks were provided in some places so that children could play their own version of these games.

D

DEODANDUM

The first accident on the infant Great Western Railway occurred in Sonning Cutting, near Reading, on Christmas Eve 1841. A mixed train of carriages and wagons ran into a landslip in the early hours of the morning, resulting in the death of eight of the passengers and serious injuries to others. At the subsequent inquest a deodand of £1,000 was placed upon the locomotive *Hecla* and the rolling stock it was hauling. Five years after this GWR accident the ancient law of deodand came to an end, but it had existed since the earliest days and was invoked in many cases in Somerset.

The concept underlying deodandum was that where a death was the fault of something other than 'any reasonable creature', that thing should be 'given to God.' In theory at least, its value passed to the monarch for redistribution to the poor. In this way the soul of the deceased would receive a roundabout intercession for the accident of having passed into purgatory unshriven. At times the deodand payment was awarded by the sheriff and distributed by the priest, and occasionally the monarch and all the faithful were intended to benefit from its benevolent use and accompanying prayers.

All sorts of items featured in the various Somerset examples. One man died from a fall in a Taunton church, resulting in a deodand of sixpence being placed on the beam from which he had fallen. In 1243 the clapper of a bell in Crewkerne church fell on Walter Knoll and killed him. It too was valued at sixpence, as was a tree branch that fell on a beggar at Wells. In contrast, a boat which was involved in a drowning at Langport realised the considerable sum of 5*s*, while a horse involved in a death at Harptree was assessed at 3*s*.

DISPUTED POUND

A number of examples of village pounds still survive in Somerset, although some are in ruinous condition and others have been absorbed into buildings or property walls. The years of land enclosure had brought an end to their

At Stogursey part of the former pound, complete with viewing slot, has survived as a garden wall.

function of housing animal strays, but for centuries earlier they had been a common and vital part of rural life.

Most pounds were square or rectangular, although the one at Hatch Beauchamp was octagonal. The surrounding stone wall would be anything from 6 to 12ft high with a single entrance, and sometimes, narrow viewing slits.

The Court Leet of the local manor appointed a pinder whose job it was to round up stray animals and confine them inside the pound until the owner could be found. If the pound was of the 'overt' type, the owner could collect his stray stock without payment. If it was a 'covert' pound, the stock owner could only reclaim his property after handing over the fixed 'turnkey' release fee. Compensation might also be required for any damage done.

The local pound was also a useful place for solving a temporary accommodation problem. At North Curry, responsibility for the pound rested for over fifty years with the village blacksmith. On one occasion it was used to house 300 geese, twenty-two turkeys and a handful of ducks; probably birds on their way to a market somewhere. A man was on duty for three days and two nights to make sure none flew over the wall and had his food, drink and tobacco brought to him. Not an enviable job, for the noise must have been near unbearable.

Small disputes involving the pinder and his pound were commonplace, and to be expected. Owners were inclined to dispute whether their animals had actually been wandering and the validity of the charges they were asked to pay.

They probably had real difficulty in keeping them on unfenced common land anyway, but the pinder had his job to do and would be expected to do it, especially if the stray animal had caused damage in the course of its roaming. One pound dispute, though, was rather more serious.

In April 1615 the tenants of the manors of Othery and Middlezoy had, in open court, agreed that the lords of the two manors could fence an area of around four acres and use it as a joint cattle pound. The scheme was duly carried out using timber posts, rails and gates with access provision for those who needed to cross the area to get to their grounds. However, this was not the end of the story. Clearly the agreement had not been completely unanimous, for 'certain turbulent and malicious persons armed with axes, saws, billhooks, and such like tools did break down the said fences on May 13th, about 9.0 of the clock at Middlesoway, and laid open the said pieces of enclosed land.'

The excuse for this dramatic action was that the enclosure was 'very dangerous and prejudicial to the freeholders' and some serious renegotiation had to take place.

DOG WHIPPERS AND OTHERS

The pews in Crowcombe church display a feast of exquisite carvings.

We would now consider the presence of dogs in church unacceptable, except in the case of blind people. But it was normal at one time, especially in communities where dogs were a part of local working life. A shepherd and his dog, for example, were a unit and a part of the Christian pattern. While the animals were well behaved this was no problem, but if their noise or strife interrupted the proceedings, the church 'dog whipper' would be called into action, aided by his whip and, possibly, tongs. Ilminster paid its dog whipper 10*s* for his services, but perhaps he had more to do than his counterpart at Nailsea, where the vestry book of 1715 reads: 'Paid Dr Lovell for whipping dogs at church 1*s* 9*d*.' A payment of half a crown was made at Axbridge in 1629 and of 2*s* at Churchstanton in 1772, but fees varied greatly according to location.

Churches and their practices all changed greatly over the centuries.

Until pews were introduced in the sixteenth century, congregations would be expected to stand, but in some cases 'shelves' were provided along the walls for the benefit of semi-invalids; hence the concept of 'weakest to the wall'. When pews were provided they had to be rented, except for a few reserved for the poor.

In 1637 one church charged 5*s* for life occupancy, another 6*d* a year. Vacant seats were usually auctioned. The seating location reflected the social order, with the more elaborate accommodation used by the rich at the front (often separate or enclosed), sometimes in a parvine above the church porch. It would be used by retainers as well as family members. The 1804 room above the porch at Selworthy was used by the Acland family, and had its own fireplace and chimney stack.

With pews reflecting the social standing of their occupants, the rows at the back were crowded, and often amounted to no more than rough benches. Men and women sat separately. There were many quarrels over pews, especially in the seventeenth century, and some churches appointed 'pew-openers' to control usage. Often women, they needed to be present at all services and could, if necessary, act as witnesses. Many churches had someone to awaken any member of the congregation who dozed off, in one case with the aid of a staff with a ball at one end and a feather at the other. Pew rentals were generally abolished by the mid-eighteenth century.

Medieval parishioners were expected to attend every Sunday morning service and could be fined if they did not. Other fines included one for 'mocking the church' when failing to proceed with a planned marriage. Before the introduction of compulsory church rates there would be a twice-yearly house collection by 'hogelers', with the proceeds going for the discharge of the churchwardens' various outgoings.

Fines for non-attendance at services began in the reign of Edward VI, with the first Act of Unification prescribing a fine of 12*d* for this, to be levied by the churchwardens and used for the benefit of the poor. There were other fines for nonconformity, and later, for not taking the Oath of Supremacy. The latter put four Minehead folk in gaol in 1683. They were not released until 1685, when they presumably made the single church attendance that would accord them one-year's immunity and an escape from the ongoing fines. In the same period, six poor people of Minehead received 2*s* each out of the fines levied on non-attenders.

Church services might be long and incomprehensible to some and the code of righteous behaviour was not to be breached lightly, but the parish church was also the centre of fun and entertainment on feast and holy days.

During the fifteenth and sixteenth centuries many parishes acquired a Church House, often built by the lord of the manor. These houses were subject to a Lord Rent which, in turn, was dispensed by the churchwardens. The former morality plays, dancing and other semi-religious activities were transferred from the church nave to the Church House, to make room for the installation of pews and an undivided emphasis on the religious service. Sometimes functioning as a poor house as well, the Church House would be used to brew the ale and bake the bread for 'church ales'; the sale of these items would contribute to church income.

There were several varieties of these 'ales'. At bride-ales a couple being married would share in the money raised; clerk-ales were designed to raise funds for the use of the parish clerk; and bid-ales were held to provide funds for the poor or some other special cause. It is believed that ale and other provisions might have been sold from the church house at Creech St Michael to boatmen on the nearby Bridgwater & Taunton Canal and the Tone Navigation. By the end of the sixteenth century, things had got a bit out of hand, so much so that at Yeovil in 1607 there were complaints about the 'minstrelaye and dauncing on Sunday'. The Assizes eventually banned all types of ales in 1631.

Church ales, collections, pew rents and donations all helped to fund the local church and its obligations, especially to the poor. Decisions on social, maintenance and other matters were made by the incumbent and the churchwardens of the vestry. The accounts of the churchwardens reveal a vast range of financial support examples, from meeting medical and burial costs to a modest handout to destitute wanderers. A major disaster might result in the issue of an official 'brief', authorising an appeal to churches in a stipulated area for financial support.

Music has always played a significant part in church life, but became less constrained in the eighteenth century. Many churches had a musicians' gallery with woodwind, viols and other instruments purchased by the churchwardens, and a pitch pipe to get the singers started. Musicians and singers were often located in the rood loft, above the rood screen. At this time, psalm-singing societies were commonplace and the more wealthy parishes might be able to pay a singing master for his services. At Over Stowey in 1807, Parson Holland complained bitterly that 'his singing gentlemen were all gone to Enmore', so not everything was always sweetness and light.

Happily, Somerset has a wide variety of churches, ranging from cathedrals, through minster and parish churches to very modest places like the atmospheric little church at Loxton. In most you can find a leaflet or small booklet explaining the features and detailing the history of the location.

DUKE'S CLOSE SHAVE

James, Duke of Monmouth, landed a small force at Lyme Regis in mid-June 1685 to spark a rising that escalated from a plan to limit the power of Catholic monarch James II into one to replace him. Gathering thinking people not only from the gentry, but also from the ranks of farmers, craftsmen and the disillusioned militia encountered in small skirmishes, the Duke's growing 'army' passed through Taunton, Bridgwater and Shepton Mallet to pause at Keynsham, in readiness for an attack on Bristol. By this time, however, the royalist forces had gathered, and their sheer numbers deterred Monmouth from an assault either on that city or on neighbouring Bath. Turning south, he headed towards Frome in order to strengthen his host before his planned march through Wiltshire and on to London. On the march south from Bath, a halt was called at Norton St Philip, where his men set up camp and the Duke and his officers retired to the George Inn.

The George Inn had originally been a guesthouse belonging to Hinton Priory whose monks also used it for the storage of wool from their large flocks of sheep. They had a charter for two major three-day fairs at which the wool was sold. Much of the business at these fairs and the weekly markets in the town would have been conducted at the George Inn. The Carthusian priory itself was sufficiently far from the inn to avoid involvement in the high spirits and occasional altercations that fair days produced.

Hinton St Philip and its notable inn went downhill for a time after Prior Horde and his monks had to bow to Dissolution in 1539. A hundred years later, we know the building was being used largely as a wool store. However, the George's hospitality function carried on and the inn was to find a special place in history in the middle of the year of the Monmouth Rebellion.

If Norton St Philip had any warning at all of the approach of the rebel army it could hardly have been prepared for the mass of mounted men, foot soldiers and battle equipment which descended on the town during the afternoon and evening of Friday 26 June 1685. The army's first job was to requisition carts, fences and gates to barricade the approaches in order to guard against possible attack by the pursuing force under Lord Feversham. That done, there were tent sites to be found, barns to be made habitable and food procured and prepared for several thousand men. In the George Inn, the turmoil outside was mirrored by the landlord and staff as they hastily provided their notable guests with food, bedrooms and somewhere to mull over the news brought in by scouts, and to formulate the plans that had to be made for dealing with the situation.

The night brought no unpleasant surprises for the pickets, but the Duke himself was to get a scare as he rose and went to shave the following morning. A strong legend maintains that, whether by accident or design, a pistol was discharged

An old view of the *George Inn* at Norton St Philip. The window through which an attempt was made on the life of the Duke of Monmouth is the one above the main entrance.

from the road below his window, the ball smashing through the glass and nearly putting an end to the mission there and then.

The day then improved for the startled and shaken Duke, with the muskets of his defenders inflicting serious casualties on Feversham's men and contributing to their eventual withdrawal after a drawn-out exchange of cannon fire in a spell of heavy rain. The rebel army could now resume its journey, and leaving bonfires burning to deceive its pursuers, left Norton St Philip and the George Inn to resume their normal modest pace of life.

Not for the first time the course of history had been at the mercy of a single, simple incident. Had the assassin's bullet found its mark, Monmouth's ill-fated venture would have ended at Norton St Philips instead of in its subsequent sad climax near Westonzoyland.

E

ELECTION FEVER

'We find that corrupt practices have extensively prevailed at the last election, and at every preceding election for the Borough of Bridgwater into which we have enquired…' This was the finding of the commissioners appointed to examine voting in Bridgwater, as recorded in their report on the Parliamentary elections which had taken place there between 1831 and 1868. In the two months of their investigation, the commissioners had examined over 500 witnesses and their eventual report added, 'We have not made out any schedule of persons treating or having been treated at the different elections into which we have inquired, because such a schedule would probably have contained the names of the greater part of the voters in the borough.'

As 2,787 votes had been cast for the four main candidates in the 1868 election and bribes were generally £10 a time, the sums of money involved were substantial. The outcome of the inquiry by the commissioners was the shame of disenfranchisement of the borough, but Bridgwater was by no means alone in some of the doubtful practices of the two main political parties, Conservative and Liberal, in the nineteenth century.

There had always been plenty of rich and well-connected candidates seeking election in Somerset, and plenty of men of influence to back them and expect benefits from doing so. Until the reform measures of 1832, the right to send members to Parliament and the right to vote in their election had not followed a uniform pattern. In some boroughs only town officials could vote; in Taunton it was 'pot-wallers not receiving alms or charity'. Quite a small number of votes could make the difference between being returned and not being returned, so the temptations to influence the result were great, and ranged from lavish entertainment to costly bribery.

Bribery became such a regular practice that it turned into an expectation, with all but a few voters seeking the maximum they could get for their support. One report expressed the cynical view that three-quarters of voters were receiving bribes and the other quarter distributing them! Not only that, but a voter's family would expect this perk to be passed on as an inheritance entitlement.

The period leading up to a vote was always a major occasion in town life, with the election agents for each candidate spending large sums on coloured ribbons, rosettes, banners or other legitimate methods of promoting their man. Public houses, especially those near the open platforms used as hustings, were gathering places for supporters, each hostelry making clear its allegiance with a display of coloured decorations of various types. Drinks were dispensed liberally, with the election agents usually picking up the bill and hiding it from official scrutiny. Candidates toured the streets, resplendent in their carriages, often accompanied by their wives and with buff or blue decorations on their vehicle, their horses and themselves to make sure that their political loyalties were not in any doubt. But behind all this fairly wholesome façade, much more sinister activities were afoot.

It was customary to arrange a banquet for selected guests with the right to vote, and the fare at these was not stinted. At Minehead in 1761 a whole buck was provided, with the best parts roasted and the remainder served in pasties. There were also huge servings of beef, ham, rabbits, sauces and the like, with a liberal supply of tarts and puddings to follow. In 1768 a bill for the spirits provided at one election event suggests that each of the eighty or so diners could have consumed over a pint of gin or brandy if they were so minded.

Elections at Minehead also reveal strong evidence of social polarisation. The less influential voters were not included among the banquet guests, but were separately entertained in public houses instead. On occasion they used their brief moment of power to act in concert and bargain for things like rent constraint, property improvement and other rewards for their vote, while in the reverse direction there seem to have been veiled threats of eviction for vote defaulters. In monetary terms the Minehead voting bribe was about a half-crown in 1734 and had 272 takers, but this figure had risen to 3 guineas by 1768.

It was at Bridgwater that the art of vote-rigging through bribery reached really remarkable heights. Aware of their power, eligible voters could expect at least £10 for their favour, but many got more than this by one means or another. The more avaricious would withhold the promise of their support until the last moment and loiter near the hustings for a better offer, which might be as much as £50 if the news from the voting procedures suggested a really close contest. Other voters might indulge in a bit of trading by offering goods for sale, but not being expected to hand them over. A pig and a parrot featured in two such cases.

Behind the scenes even more devious events were taking place. At one end of the spectrum would be the candidate and men of some influence in the area, all intent on keeping their hands clean, although they must have known that the massive cost incurred would ultimately come from their own purses. Each candidate would have an agent, or 'introducer'; often a person who

The former *Royal Clarence Hotel* was a focal point for Bridgwater social, political and business activity. Right from its opening in 1825 it set out to cater for every need as shown by advertising which claimed, it possessed 'every advantage', including the availability of 'Neat Landaus, Post Chaises, Chaises, a Hearse, Mourning Coaches.' *(Roy Gallop)*

would have masterminded the seamy side of campaigns elsewhere. Down the line would be so-called 'inferior agents', frequently tradesmen or innkeepers. And right at grass roots there was a shadowy character loitering in a darkened back room of a hostelry issuing the bribes in return for proof of the right to vote, sometimes a marked card, and then making an appropriate record in his notebook. Bridgwater knew this person as 'The Man in the Moon', and the money packets he handed over might be referred to as packets of tea or something equally innocuous.

In fact, voting bribes were normally in the form of golden sovereigns. In a typical situation the introducer would weigh up what sum might be needed to secure a favourable result, check with a senior intermediary that his candidate was willing to pay it and then head off to a bank with a cheque to be cashed. The return journey was made with a bag full of sovereigns, which another secretive figure would collect to be sorted and packeted up for the bribery activity. In the run up to voting, as facts and rumours were fed back up the chain, furtive discussions would take place in lawyers' offices, clubs or hotel rooms to decide how to achieve the desired outcome and to hide its costs from public scrutiny. In Bridgwater, both the Globe at Eastover and the New Inn nearby were deeply involved in the bribery business.

Not surprisingly, elections were highly charged affairs often provoking violence. The period surrounding the Reform Bill of 1832 was the most volatile, with the Riot Act having to be read in a number of locations and a lot of property being damaged by mobs of various persuasions. A mock burial of one candidate in Bridgwater cannot have helped, and the editor of a newly launched newspaper was one of the sufferers when a mob wrecked his house and emptied his cellar. Similar events took place in Yeovil, where the homes of several notable figures were ransacked and vandalised. The Lamb Inn at Axbridge was subjected to what was labelled as a 'felonious, unlawful and riotous attack'.

Like Bridgwater and Minehead, Ilchester was another town with a disturbing election history. With only 100 or so ratepayers entitled to vote, cash bribery was not too daunting a financial proposition, although the going rate had risen to £30 before the end of the eighteenth century. Money could also persuade the returning officer to mislay votes. Buying up property to achieve ratepayer status was another device used, but possibly the worst example of malpractice was that of the demolition of homes liable to vote the wrong way and forcing their occupiers into the workhouse.

The problems in Bridgwater were not confined to 1831 and 1832, but went on and on. The by-election of May 1837 was no exception, and the outcome was so significant that *The Times* arranged a relay of horses to speed the news to London. After the Conservative candidate had been returned, the Liberals were able to substantiate 153 accusations of bribery, but then lost again in the following contest by a masterly piece of trickery. In this instance a number of people were bribed not only to vote Tory, but also to convince the Liberal agent of their support for his principal so that he decided bribery on his part was unnecessary! In 1859 around 500 voters who had been bribed to vote Conservative were given another £10 by the Liberal agent and then carefully herded to the hustings on election morning.

These bad practices were prevalent in Bridgwater for over thirty years, with most elections being followed by a complaint from the unsuccessful candidates. After the 1865 election, the petition from the losing Liberal candidates was heard by a Parliamentary Select Committee, but after the 1868 elections it was the Conservative petition that had the winning Liberals unseated. This situation could not continue and the result was the setting up of the commission to investigate and report on what was going on in Bridgwater. Its report, stretching to over 1,000 pages, made dramatic reading and resulted in the town's loss of the franchise.

Slowly over the years the supervision of elections improved. The old bribery habit suffered a major setback when the secret ballot was introduced in 1872. With the extension of the franchise in 1884 to all men over twenty-one years of age, the roles of the introducer, the inferior agent and the Man in the Moon finally became redundant.

‘ELECTRICIAN’ CROSSE

In 1836, at the pleasant, quiet, but unlikely village of Broomfield, 6 miles east of Taunton, a situation occurred that was to create a major stir in scientific and religious circles. At his Quantock home at Fyne Court, fifty-two-year-old Andrew Crosse had been experimenting with the interaction between chemicals and electricity for producing crystals for some time. Now, his processes were to produce results so startling as to provoke the nation into hot debate and the press into rather more excited reporting than was usual. These results were to earn him the label of ‘The Electrician’ among other, often less flattering, references.

Andrew Crosse had been born in 1784 into an affluent family and had enjoyed the privileges of travel and an excellent education. He had responded with a display of application and talent in areas as diverse as the arts, nature and science, with the novelty of electricity growing into a lifelong interest. The death of parents Richard and Susan brought the family home and estates to Andrew at the young age of twenty-one, when he gave up law studies to manage them. This gave him the means and freedom to pursue his wide interests and purchase the equipment he needed to do so.

By all accounts Andrew Crosse was a quiet, sensible man, whose scientific researches were thoughtful and meticulous. He was respected by his peers and in no way given to boasting, exaggeration or seeking the limelight. But his work was to produce a dramatic result that leaked out and got widely reported, mostly adversely. All sorts of accusations were levelled at Crosse, especially by church interests, and even 100 years later articles appeared in both *The Times* and *Tit Bits* labelling him ‘the man who “made” insects.’ The way of it was this.

In the grounds of Fyne Court, Crosse had rigged up a huge network of wires to enable him to harness natural electricity in Leyden Jars. By all accounts this was a dramatic process, producing loud reports and flashes of light, which gave rise to another description of Crosse as ‘the thunder and lightning man.’ Passing the home-made electric current through various chemical solutions, he experimented for some time, developing methods of producing various types of crystals. In 1836 he was working on trying to obtain silica this way. Eventually, he used a mixture of powdered flint and potassium carbonate, fusing these compounds in a furnace. The powder obtained was dissolved in boiling water, hydrochloric acid was added, and the resultant fluid used to saturate a porous stone ready to receive a charge of electricity.

It was a variation of this process that led to seemingly incredible results. Nothing out of the ordinary happened for the first fourteen days. Crosse then noticed a few tiny white spots on the stone he had used, but still had no inkling of what was to follow. Four days later he found the spots larger and with tiny 'bristles' projecting from them. By day twenty-six, raised up on these were what appeared to be tiny insects. Four weeks into this remarkable scenario the incredulous Andrew Crosse then observed life and movement among the creatures he had 'created'. Even more of the mites followed, some, curiously, with six legs and others with eight.

Not given to making hasty assumptions, Crosse thought that the stone he had used must have contained ova which had been stimulated by his processes, but repeating the experiment with every effort to produce sterile conditions led to precisely the same result. Experts called upon to examine Crosse's 'creatures' believed them to belong to the Acarus genus and honoured him by calling his particular strain Acarus Crossii.

'The Electrician' made no claims or fuss about this startling series of experiments. Indeed he proved very reluctant to advise even his close friends and chosen scientific associates, but the news got out and a furore erupted. Local people, in particular, were angered by what they saw as both threatening and interfering with nature. So much so that some went to the extreme of arranging an exorcism. Religious opinion as a whole was, understandably, at the best sceptical and often incensed. The response by Crosse was to state that he merely reported what had happened and that any conclusions to be drawn he would leave to others.

The Fyne Court 'insects' failed to survive the frosts of winter and other attempts to replicate the manner of their creation mostly failed. The controversy they had caused eventually perished as well and it seems likely that its root cause lay in ova in the stones used in the experiments that the sterility precautions of the day had failed to eradicate.

Fyne Court itself suffered a major fire in 1898, forty-three years after its controversial owner had died, but the grounds remain available for public enjoyment under National Trust ownership and also provide a home for the Somerset Wildlife Trust.

EMPEROR'S DAUGHTER IN A SOMERSET HAYSTACK

A chapbook of 1785 recounted a rather peculiar story under the title of 'The Wandering Young Lady'.

The young lady in question was supposedly Louisa, a natural daughter of the Austrian Emperor Francis I and one who, for some undisclosed reason, was abandoned by the family after the emperor's death. A portrait of her is said to have been painted by W. Palmer, but the account of her supposed four years spent in a haystack near Flax Bourton, as recounted below, takes some believing:

> In the latter part of the eighteenth century, a young girl of refined and elegant appearance and manners, forlorn and demented, took shelter beneath an old haystack, and made it her home for four years, refusing to exchange it for any other abode. She declined all assistance beyond the barest necessaries of life, nor would she communicate her antecedents to anyone. She became at length an inmate of an asylum at Bitton from whence she was transferred, by the kindness of Miss Hannah More, to a similar institution in London, where she died in 1800 and her sad story with her.

EXMOOR'S 3,300FT INCLINE

Hidden away in Eastern Wood on a steep slope of the Brendon Hills are remnants of a near-forgotten, but quite remarkable, industry. Minerals had been mined on the higher ground and on the plain immediately below for many years, but the original pattern of small, low-output sites was to change dramatically in the middle of the nineteenth century. At that time the ironmasters of South Wales were demanding increasing quantities of ore for their furnaces and, when the Brendon workings were surveyed and proved to contain workable deposits of good quality ore, the Brendon Hills Iron Co. was formed in 1853 to exploit them. The problem was getting the ore from high on the hills down to the port of Watchet and the ships which would then convey it on to Newport for the final stage of the journey to the hungry furnaces of Ebbw Vale.

The company's solution was the West Somerset Mineral Railway, for which they obtained an authorising Act of Parliament in 1855. It was planned that the line would take a modestly graded route inland to Comberow and then gain some 800ft in height by a bold incline of 1 in 4 to reach the summit. From there it would continue west to the mines around Gupworthy, with a branch in the opposite direction to serve the Raleigh's Cross mine. No time was lost and by April 1857 the new railway was open between Watchet and Roadwater.

The WSMR now concentrated on completing the lower section on to Comberow and then the 3,300ft stretch up through the wood to the summit near Raleigh's Cross. Although it made use of the natural course of a tiny stream, the incline was a major undertaking requiring, in some places, the excavation of cuttings through the solid rock and, in others, using the resultant debris to build up embankments. The work was hard and expensive, but despite this, the double line of standard gauge track which had reached Comberow by the end of 1857 had been extended to the top of the incline by mid-1858. The through route still needed some finishing touches, but the first loads of ore could now move by rail instead of making the long and difficult journey down the hill by horse-drawn vehicle.

The engine house at the top of the West Somerset Mineral Railway incline, as it was in 1976.

The railway incline breasted the summit onto an embankment into which was set a substantial masonry building to house the engine and twin drums required to haul wagons up the steep 3,300ft-long incline.

There were huge problems in shipping the 18ft drums over from Newport, getting them to the top of the hill, and then manoeuvring them into position. Until the work was finally completed in 1861 it seems that some temporary steam power was used, along with as much counterbalancing as could be achieved by linking descending loads with ascending empties.

In their best years the Brendon Hill mines were sending up to twenty wagons of ore down the incline every day, usually one wagon at a time, under the control of a brakeman who had a hut at the top of the slope. Once Comberow station had signalled its readiness, he would attach the descending wagon to the cable emerging from the winding house, release the friction brake which acted on the drum, and then engage the engine. There was at least one case of wagons running downhill out of control, but they became derailed and, thankfully, failed to complete the descent.

A substantial community of miners, railway staff and ancillary workers was soon established around the top of the incline along with housing, schooling, churches and stores for supplies. Goods for the community went up the incline in the same way as the empty ore wagons, and an informal service for passengers was provided by fitting one vehicle with crude seats. By 1865 a proper passenger train service was running between Watchet and Comberow, where people changed for the less conventional but rather more dramatic ascent of the hill.

Changes in demand, technology and ore availability made iron ore mining an insecure business, and the end of the 1870s heralded a period of recession that was eventually to close the mines down and end the working on the incline. The railway service on the lower section hung on until 1898 and there was a brief revival in the mining activity in 1907, but this lasted only a short time and nature began to reclaim the great, stark and once-busy railway trackbed which climbed the Brendon Hills from Comberow.

F

FATHERLY FLOGGING

In 1829 one issue of the *Taunton Courier* carried the following report:

> A young lad, the son of a toll keeper near Langport, being occasionally employed in the absence of his father, to receive the tolls, contrived last week to get at the money box, from which he helped himself very abundantly for the purpose of gambling and 'pitch and toss' for half crowns, with two farmers' boys in the neighbourhood. The father at last detected the depredator, and made the farmer acquainted with the conduct of the two young boys who encouraged him to robbery. The farmer conceiving that the imprisonment (of) two young offenders among practised and hardened old ones, would only plant corruption more deeply in their minds, contended [*sic*] himself with threatening to send them instantly to gaol, unless they would agree to obey his orders. These were that they should tie each up by turns to the turnpike-gate, and flog each other soundly with a good ground ash stick. The lads preferred this alternative to confinement in a gaol, and belaboured each other in right earnest until the farmer was satisfied.
>
> It was now the toll keeper's turn, who, tying up his son in the same manner, flogged him with such severity, that the farmer thought proper to interfere on his behalf with his exasperated father. All the inhabitants of the neighbouring village, and several gentlemen travelling on the road, witnessed the administering of this wholesome discipline. There are thousands of instances like the above, in which the infliction of sound corporal punishment would be far preferable to imprisonment, and deter youth from prosecuting a career which is sure to lead to an ignominious end.

FIVES, THE FORGOTTEN GAME

In South Somerset, several imposing high walls (often referred to as 'towers') still bear witness to a game that was extremely popular in the county for many years, but is now largely forgotten. The game was 'fives', a sort of outdoor squash that graduated from informal contests using a wall of the local church, to structured competitions with purpose-built 'towers' and celebrated players.

In one form or another, fives has probably been about for a long time, but the first mention of it in Somerset is at Williton in the 1630s. Played against the church wall there, it was already provoking complaint from the churchwardens, a feature which later reappeared at Wrington where the church windows were regularly falling victim to enthusiastic but inaccurate fives players. At Montacute the vicar put a stop to their activities by having the base of the village cross dumped on the playing area. Several Somerset churches were fitted with window shutters to minimise the damage caused by devotees of the increasingly popular game.

Fives caused serious trouble at Martock, where the churchwardens' accounts make lengthy reference to the game, first in 1740 and then in 1754, when there was a clear intention 'to prevent fives playing in the south side of ye church.' Four years later, it provoked the comment: 'it having been found to be the occasion of much mischief being done to the windows of the Church, also to the leads and walls of it, and also of much wickedness causing swearing, quarrelling and fighting in the Churchyard.'

However, the game had such a hold on the young men of Martock that it continued to cause problems, not least because one player had suffered a fractured skull, caused by falling masonry dislodged by someone climbing to retrieve a lost ball from the roof. Again the preventative measures were drastic, 'digging a ditch across ye fives place' no less, and costing church funds of 3*s* 6*d*.

Around this time fives players began to see the writing on their church wall, as it were, and purpose-built walls began to appear. An 1808 painting by George Bennett of 'The Fives Wall and Mrs Gallopp's Cottage, Axbridge Hill' shows a date of 1757 on the wall itself. It also shows the players in rather unlikely formal dress. Soon, walls were being built adjacent to popular inns, mostly in stone and usually flanked by narrow buttresses, in imitation of the traditional church wall. A fine wall survives at the Lord Poulett Arms at Hinton St George with another at the Fleur-de-Lys at Stoke-sub-Hamdon.

The height of this 'fives wall' at the *Lord Poulett Arms* at Hinton St George gives some idea of the demands the game would have made on its players.

There are also walls still standing near the former Crown Inn at South Petherton and the New Inn at Shepton Beauchamp, and the remains of one at The Bell at Curry Rivel. The general pattern is of a well-built and finished stone structure some 30ft high and 20ft wide, usually with buttresses, and sometimes decorative finials. Plainer brick walls were used at the Lethbridge Arms at Bishops Lydeard and the Anchor Inn at Combwich.

This imposing 'fives wall' survives from the closure of the *Crown Inn* at South Petherton.

The fives game also flourished at schools such as Eton and Winchester, but the version played there called for hitting the ball onto specified areas of the wall. In Somerset, both Sexey's School at Bruton and Ilchester Grammar School had walls. Another version required the ball to be bounced, struck and returned from the wall onto the starting square, but yet other forms were more similar to squash, with each player or team trying to best the other with the speed and variety achieved on the return of strike. The name may derive from scoring in multiples of five.

At the height of the fives era there was considerable competition between popular players and teams. In one notable game at the Fleur-de-Lys, the two star players of Stoke-sub-Hamdon, John Palmer and Frederick Fame, took on a pair from Bath and beat them soundly before a large number of spectators accommodated on a special grandstand, having paid £60 in 'gate money'. During the match Palmer made one especially memorable strike. The ball was bounced on the serving square let into the ground some 20ft in front of the wall, struck mightily by the player with his bare hand and rebounded from the wall with such force that it cleared the spectators' stand in what is now the pub's beer garden and landed on the roof.

Fives continued to enjoy great popularity and support well into the nineteenth century. It clearly had a significant and organised following in South Somerset, but the more modest local games played against church walls continued, leading Parson Holland to record in his diary for 31 May 1807, 'Two boys played at fives against the church wall (at Dodington) while the bell was tolling and I soon routed them off.' Although the wall at Ilminster Grammar School blew down around 1896, fives was still being played at Sexey's as late as the 1950s. There seems little doubt that Somerset's forgotten game lasted for around three centuries altogether and was played in some thirty locations in the county at one time or another.

FOSCOTT MAIDS

A worn effigy in the parish church of Norton St Philip depicts two young girls who have become known as the Fair Maids of Foscott. But it's a sad story if the information in the writings of the Revd Collinson is to be believed. The two girls were Siamese twins who lived for a number of years before one of the pair died and, according to Collinson, 'the survivor was constrained to drag about her lifeless companion till death released her of her horrid burden.' Their burial at Norton St Philip must have represented a merciful end to an incredibly unhappy saga.

Another Somerset example of Siamese twins highlights the sad fact that for many centuries, the fate of any person born with abnormalities was either an early demise or a life of being treated as a spectacle. Of one such case in the 1680s one writer commented, 'Their birth, being thus with their bodies strangely united, hath proved very much Advantageous to their parents, by the numerous Access of the Multitude, who come to see the Children from many miles round about, and give the parents considerably.'

After giving birth to three perfectly normal children, a woman of Isle Brewers again became pregnant. She had been less than well for a while and then suffered the premature arrival of two conjoined baby girls. The twins shared a common trunk from armpits to hip bones, but had separate heads and lower limbs. By all accounts the two girls had distinct personalities and even slept at different times.

How these Isle Brewers twins came to be called Aquila and Priscilla is a mystery, and hints at some external influences. They lived long enough to be exploited for financial gain by unscrupulous people who arranged for them to be exhibited to the curious in return for a cash payment. Such was the practice of the times.

FROME'S BLIND HOUSE

St John's Church at Frome is not a gloomy place, although it does have a masonry depiction of the *Via Crucis* to one side and a small, dark churchyard on the other. And right in the darkest corner of the latter, half submerged and dwarfed by the sombre grey stone of the churchyard wall, is the former blind house. The cramped, damp and dark chamber was used to house the town's wrongdoers at one period, and a night in there after an evening of excessive revelry must have caused many to deeply regret the error of their ways. The town had a second facility in the former guardhouse beside the town bridge, but this no longer exists.

The attractive looking lock-up building at Bailey Hill, Castle Cary would not have held the same appeal to those confined inside.

Blind houses, more commonly referred to as lock-ups, were a feature of most sizeable communities before the emergence of an organised police force with proper police stations and cells on the premises. They supplanted the earlier practice of parish constables having to keep anyone they arrested secure, often in their own homes, prior to appearance before the local magistrate the following morning. As they were used only for short stay confinement, there was no call for amenities and without exception, they were dismal and uncomfortable places at best.

Along with Wiltshire, Somerset has more surviving examples of lock-ups than any other part of the country. Many are separate buildings, others part of a civic building or market house. Most of the stand alone structures are square or rectangular, but Somerset is also blessed with rare examples of round and octagonal buildings. The Round House standing at Bailey Hill, Castle Cary, for example, is a good-looking circular lock-up which was provided in 1779 and cost £23.

There is an apocryphal story that one occupant froze to death there at Christmas, and certainly there was a School Committee ruling in 1785 that children playing truant could be confined there, although it is doubtful if this ever happened. Slightly less spartan provision for confinement was made within the town's new market house when it was built in 1855.

Drunkenness, vagrancy, theft or profanity were the most common reasons for confinement in a lock-up, but the one at Nether Stowey was once put to a rather different use. On that occasion a foreigner arrived there with his performing bear and, although this occurrence was not all that unusual for the time, the local inhabitants were not happy about the bear being in the town overnight and so shut the animal and its owner in the lock-up. Contrary to some expectations both emerged unscathed in the morning.

Miscreants often refused to take lightly being locked in an unpleasant cell. The rowdy drunks made a lot of noise, aided sometimes by their cronies. Lock-up roofs were never made of wood or prisoners could have broken out or been rescued, but this did not stop 'comforts' being supplied to them through a grill or ventilation slot. There is even one account of a woman fetching a pot of beer for her man and supplying it through the lock-up keyhole by using the long stem of a 'churchwarden's' pipe!

G

GIANTS AND DWARVES

The nineteenth century saw many unusually tall and unusually small people appearing in menageries and other travelling shows. It was the era of well-known characters like Tom Thumb, who was only 25ins tall when he came to England in 1844 and toured around in his blue and white carriage pulled by Shetland ponies. In Somerset there was a young Taunton lady named Widdicombe who was 'proclaimed as the most impressive female dwarf ever presented to the public.' Among her public appearances was a rather special one in 1819 when members of the Royal Family marvelled at the diminutive figure who, although only 35ins tall, could bend her fingers back until they touched her elbow. In contrast, an 1886 photograph in the possession of Porlock Museum depicts a local child, Ernest Middleton, who when only one year old was taller than Miss Widdicombe by an inch. He weighed 58lb and had a 30in chest and doubtless grew to an impressive size.

Somerset has several associations with other larger-than-usual characters, including a tall skeleton whose remains were found manacled to the gatehouse at Dunster Castle and Sir John Loe whose memorial in Chew Magna church represents him as over 7ft tall. There are accounts of the remains of a 13ft giant discovered at Wedmore in 1670 and of one unearthed in Loxton churchyard whose torso alone measured 6ft 3ins, but the details are vague and unauthenticated.

A 'giantess' put in an appearance at the Assize Fair at Taunton in 1811 and another, described as 'a Somerset girl taller than any man in England', was exhibited at London's Bartholomew Fair in 1825. Said to be 6ft 11ins tall, sixteen years old and named Elizabeth Stock, part of this extraordinary young person's act involved handing her slippers to the biggest men in the audience and inviting them to put their booted feet inside. Around the same time, at least one other tall Somerset lady from the Crewkerne area was appearing on the exhibition circuit.

A Lincolnshire giant, Joseph Neal Sewell, was charitably befriended at Taunton when his life was at its lowest ebb. Such was the help and kindness he received that before his death in July 1829 Sewell several times expressed a strong wish to be brought back to Taunton for burial. The 7ft 4in giant, who weighed thirty-seven stone, feared that his abnormal body would be misused after his death and believed that he could only trust the town that had offered him help to ensure this did not happen. In due course his patrons in Taunton faithfully responded to his wishes and arranged for the giant's interment in St Mary Magdalen churchyard, with tradesman John Bluett apparently paying for the burial.

Joseph's story is a harrowing one, only redeemed by the kindness he received in Taunton and at Exeter. He had been born near Horncastle in Lincolnshire, but was illegitimate and very soon had to make his own way in the world by exhibiting his unusually large body wherever he could find people willing to pay for the experience. Around his twenty-first birthday, the young giant suffered a cruel blow when he caught typhus in Swansea, an illness that robbed him of his sight and compelled him to rely on the poorhouse to keep him alive. When he left there he wandered 'blind, feeble and almost helpless' first to Bristol and then south through Somerset to Taunton.

Sewell's luck took a turn for the better in Taunton where, as the *Taunton Courier* subsequently reported: 'his melancholy condition attracted the attention of some benevolent persons, who liberally administered to his necessities, and eventually enabled him to proceed to Exeter, where he was furnished with a caravan, in which to exhibit himself, and provided with a person named Broomsgrove to attend him.'

The latter operated a small menagerie so that, housed comfortably in the caravan paid for by public subscription in Exeter, the giant managed to make a reasonable living by exhibiting himself to the curious, his huge frame appearing even more remarkable by contrast when he teamed up with a 37in Somerset dwarf named Farnham.

Sewell's public appearances eventually took him back to his old haunts in Swansea, but he was never completely well, and after a series of fits, he died there. He had repeatedly expressed his great fear that, because of his unusual size, his remains would be 'exposed to anatomical operations after his death.' The giant was insistent that his body should be returned to Taunton for interment because he believed

A Roy Gallop drawing of Joseph Sewell's huge slippers, made with the permission of Taunton Museum.

that the kindnesses he had received there would extend to the anonymity of his final resting place. Faithful to his friend's wishes, Broomsgrove, a Taunton man himself, duly brought the dead giant back to the town where he had received so much help.

Joseph Sewell's fears had not been without foundation, for Broomsgrove had been approached several times on his sad journey through Gloucester and Bristol to Taunton with the body of his former companion lying in the caravan. One of the most persistent offers for the remains of his friend came from a Frenchman who wanted to whisk the corpse away to Paris and was both 'extremely importunate' and 'very lavish in his offers'. But the faithful Broomsgrove had turned down all the approaches and attracted the praise of the newspaper for 'having done his duty to the deceased.' Sewell's fellow performer, the dwarf Farnham, paid his respects by following the body of his companion as it passed through the crowds of Taunton folk on its final journey to the church. There, the exact location of the grave was kept a secret and quicklime used to ensure that the nightmare that had haunted Joseph Sewell would never be realised.

Another giant, supposedly born in Patagonia in the fifteenth century, deserves mention for his forty-five-year connection with Somerset. Kap Dwa, as this unusual man was called, was 12ft tall and had two heads, and the sight of his preserved body was well known to visitors to Weston-super-Mare in the first half of the twentieth century. For *2d* they could marvel at the giant reclining in his case, his dark body clad in a loin cloth with a club in his hand and a serpent coiled upon his chest.

After being exhibited around the country, Kap Dwa had been brought to Somerset by a Worle man and put on display at Birnbeck Pier. Medical men who examined him found no reason to suspect deception and thought it possible that two embryo bodies had been linked vertically instead of the more-normal horizontal connection between Siamese twins. After moving 'home' to the Grand Pier, Kap Dwa eventually passed into other hands in 1959 and subsequently appeared first at Blackpool's Museum of Curiosities and then with the travelling show of 'Lord' Thomas Howard who sold him to a relative in the USA. In 1999 the giant was reputedly on tour with Billy Hill's 'white bus' when it visited Newcastle, but there the story seems to end.

'GREAT TUMULT' AT TAUNTON

On 19 May 1634 the Mayor of Taunton wrote to his monarch, Charles I, in a state of great concern about a troublesome situation in his town. Discontent had been evident for several days and had reached a head on the previous

Saturday, a busy market day attended by large numbers of people. The evidence of the discontent had been so noisy and threatening that the mayor recorded in his anxious communication that 'a great tumult was like to have been made.' The reason for his apprehension was, of all things, a glut of farthings.

At the time, the type and availability of coinage was a haphazard affair and in Taunton in 1634 there were virtually no higher value coins to be had. Every type of transaction was being conducted in farthings or farthing tokens, not only buying and selling, but also the payment of wages and similar regular settlements. This was also an era when counterfeiting was commonplace, despite the most stringent legal penalties. A rumour had spread around Taunton that many of the farthings were foreign counterfeits, which fuelled the suspicion and panic already aroused. As the doubts and discontentment escalated, people began to wonder whether the coins being offered to them were legitimate and started refusing to accept them, knowing that they would in turn face rejection when they tried to use them.

One of the consequences of this situation was that normal transactions could not be made and people could not even buy food. In his letter the mayor gave voice to this aspect, reporting that 'poor people are not able to provide themselves with necessaries for their livelihood', adding his strong concern that they 'would be like to perish, unless some speedy course be taken for their relief.'

The outcome of this situation is not known, but it seems to be a rare example of dissidence caused by something as simple as too many farthings being serious enough to be reported to the monarch.

H

HARBOUR DREAM

In 1866 a company prospectus was issued for a scheme to construct a harbour at the end of Brean Down, the limestone promontory just south of Weston-super-Mare where the Mendip range sinks into the Bristol Channel. The 1.5-mile long, 320ft high stretch of Brean Down offers secure shelter from winds and rough water, something countless sea captains had taken advantage of over the centuries on their journeys to and from Bristol and other ports of the Severn Estuary. Even so, the prospectus contained a reminder that '... shipwrecks and disasters at sea frequently occur in that locality for want of a Harbour of Refuge, while passenger and trading communication ... on either side of the Severn is necessarily interrupted and uncertain.'

Its suitability as the site for a secure harbour had been in the minds of the Wyndham family when they purchased Brean Down back in the eighteenth century, but the concept was to achieve no reality until well into the nineteenth. It was then advocated in 1841 by two eminent witnesses before a House of Commons Select Committee considering the overseas mail business.

In the 1850s there were two schemes to provide improved facilities for the cross-channel coal vessels and other traffic traditionally handled at Uphill Pill, where Brean Down rises from beside the mouth of the River Axe. These, however, were soon displaced when the Brean Down Harbour Co. was incorporated in 1861, with the intention of making the old idea of a major new port at the seaward end of the down into a reality.

On 23 October 1861 the company's engineer reported in favour of the scheme, confirming that there was an adequate depth of water at the lowest tide, a good clay bottom and excellent shelter from rough seas. In the following year the company secured its enabling Act of Parliament, which authorised the construction of a pier and harbour at the seaward end of Brean Down.

By 1864 sufficient funds had been raised to allow construction tenders to be placed. To celebrate, Lady Wilmot, the wife of the chairman of the company, presided over a ceremony on 5 November 1864 in which a foundation stone was lowered into the waters off the site from the small steamer *Wye*. Cheering, gunfire, music, prayers, feasting and fireworks marked the occasion, but the celebration was slightly marred by the stone later being carried off into the Bristol Channel by the tide acting on its buoy.

In 1865, the Brean Down Harbour Railways Act authorised the company to build a short railway line from the end of the down to the Bristol to Taunton railway line near Uphill. Construction work on the harbour itself commenced on 6 February. The powers for the connecting railway were transferred to the Bristol & Exeter Railway in 1866, a year in which the harbour company issued a detailed prospectus. This showed that the B&E was committed to building a double line of mixed gauge and allowing the harbour company a 7.5 per cent 'rebate' on the traffic it carried. This was confidently expected to include large quantities of coal brought over from South Wales, and agricultural produce in the reverse direction.

More ambitiously, the infant harbour company expected a sizeable flow of livestock traffic from Ireland and on by rail to London. It also boasted of being a slightly shorter distance to New York where, it was stated, a company was being formed to operate steamships on the route. Significantly, the Brean Down Company had as its deputy chairman Rear Admiral Sir William Hall, who was also a director of the P&O shipping company. Another BDH director

Hopes are high as a foundation stone is lowered over the side of the paddle steamer *Wye* but the dream of a fine harbour at the end of Brean Down was not to be. (*Illustrated London News*)

was chairman of the Brecon & Merthyr Tydfil Junction Railway. The company offered 36,500 shares of £10 each, to raise £125,000 for the harbour works and £240,000 for the docks.

The two engineers appointed for the Brean Down Harbour project were Joseph Cubitt and Robert May. According to a contemporary drawing there was to be a long curving breakwater carrying a double line of railway. The latter then curved round the end of Brean Down and into a tunnel before continuing along the lower northern slopes of the promontory, heading towards the mouth of the River Axe, which was to be bridged. The drawing also shows what appears to be a separate passenger station at the harbour end.

Despite some construction work being carried out, things did not go well for the harbour development. A B&E Act of 1868 extended the railway powers for another three years, but provided that if no progress on the main harbour scheme had been achieved within two, work on the line need not be started. The harbour company had to admit that 'by reason of storms and other causes, no effective progress had been made', and sought an extension of time in its own further Act in 1869. Among the 'other causes' were a series of personality disagreements and a fatal accident which befell the main contractor. To all intents and purposes, all harbour activity had come to an end by this time, a situation which seemed final when a fierce storm in 1872 undid most of the modest construction work which had been achieved.

There was now another long gap before the project was revived in 1887 and again gathered momentum both locally and in New York. The outcome was a new Brean Down Harbour & Docks Act of 1889, which reauthorised the construction of the dock and railway. Clearly there was a potential problem in acquiring the necessary lands from Sir William Wyndham, for of the seven years allowed for completion of the whole project, three were stipulated as the time limit for the land acquisition. In yet another Act of 1893 these land powers were extended to six years but, significantly, this measure provided for a £2,996 deposit which was to be paid out to injured landowners if the main scheme was not completed. This does seem to have been a touch of pessimism in the statute which, unfortunately, turned out to be well justified.

It is probably significant that the Great Western Railway tunnel under the River Severn had opened in 1886, followed by the completion of the new harbour at Milford Haven in October 1889, both taking away some of the reasons for the Brean Down facility. In any event the harbour project was not to prosper and was soon to be marked only by some minor walling of the quay base and a few blocks of dressed stone. Wave-battered and abandoned, these epitomised the dreams of the harbour's promoters and their delusions of vast quantities of the transatlantic passengers, Welsh coal and Irish cattle which they had hoped would make their fortunes.

HEADLESS SAINT

A little way outside Watchet, between the main approach road to the town and the modest Washford River, stands the church of St Decuman. It is a small but pleasing place, standing on slightly higher ground at the end of a short approach lane, and displaying an attractive perpendicular tower with some other features dating back to the thirteenth century. Although the site had been of religious significance from much earlier times, the present building represents a fifteenth and sixteenth century rebuild of an earlier Norman church.

Nearby, nestling amid natural greenery, is a spring known as St Decuman's Well. The simple well produces clear water which has a reputation for healing that also goes back to the earliest times. In particular, it was once supposed to help cure scurvy, the unpleasant affliction which resulted from diet deficiencies and was the curse of seamen deprived of fresh fruit during long voyages. The seamen of Watchet itself would have been among the sufferers who sought relief in the waters of St Decuman's well.

The Decuman who gave his name to both church and well was born in the seventh century in Rhoscrowther in Pembrokeshire. He is said to have come from a noble family, but for some reason felt the need to join the flow of Welsh Christians who believed themselves called to take their message and beliefs across the Bristol Channel to Somerset. Whether prompted by the completion of their objectives at home or despairing of doing so, we do not know. Decuman – later St Decuman – duly landed somewhere near Dunster, established a base camp with a cow for company and began his ministry.

Clearly what the Welshman had to say was not to everyone's liking, however. One listener, described as 'more venomous than an asp, more poisonous than an adder' and apparently believing that actions spoke louder than words, expressed his viewpoint by severing Decuman's head. That holy man promptly responded by picking up the errant head, washing the blood from it with the waters of the well, and then placing it back in its proper place on his shoulders.

This well at Watchet was part of the legend of St Decuman.

This miracle so impressed the people living in the small coastal community that they built a small church on the spot and the feast day of St Decuman became a regular part of the Christian calendar.

HIGHBRIDGE HERO

A modest statue in a modest town pays tribute to a little-known Somerset hero. The town is Highbridge, and the statue honours Frank Edward Foley, who was born there on 24 November 1884. Into the seventy-three years of his life that followed, Frank Foley was to cram an extraordinary range of activities and achievements: trainee priest, teacher, soldier, spy master, and a very special role as the 'British Schindler'. In this latter capacity Frank Foley saved thousands of Jews from Nazi persecution, and earned richly deserved memorials not only in his hometown, but also in London, Berlin and Israel.

The son of a railway worker, young Frank's early ability earned him a scholarship to a Jesuit college in Lancashire, and then on to a seminary in France. Transferring to academic studies he travelled around Europe, but had to make a dramatic escape at the outbreak of the First World War using disguises and clandestine boat trips to get back to England. There he joined up, was commissioned and fought in France before a bullet in the lung ended his fighting days.

By 1918 Frank Foley had been recruited into the Intelligence Corps and was running a network of secret agents in France and the Low Countries, then moving to France and subsequently on to a job in the Control Commission set up after the Armistice. The next step in the remarkable career of this remarkable man saw him in Berlin, where his official position was that of passport control officer in the British Embassy. This was a cover under which Foley carried out his work for MI6, namely that of gathering information, especially about spies who might be planning to enter Britain.

Jonathan Sells' statue of Major Frank Foley bears the inscription, 'He saved thousands of Jews from Nazi persecution'.

The priest-cum-academic-cum-soldier was now a spymaster and, whether encouraged officially or not, he took on another role that was to mean salvation for many. It was the time of Hitler's rise to power and of the persecution of Jews which followed. The applications for visas flooded in to Frank Foley's 'daytime' job. Hundreds, and then thousands, sought to escape the Nazi brutality and flee to England. Frank took the most liberal view of the control regulations to allow as many as possible to do so. He went further, visiting concentration camps to seek plausible cases for the issue of life-saving visas and risking his own freedom in the process. If necessary, this Highbridge lad was not above issuing a forged passport or even hiding a fugitive in his own home. Little wonder that Israel was subsequently to award him the status of 'Righteous Among the Nations' for this herculean task of mercy.

Brought back to London when the Second World War began, Frank Foley was one of the men chosen to question Rudolf Hess after his flight from Germany. His exceptional talents and experience were then put to use co-ordinating the efforts to run a network of double agents. Even after the end of hostilities, he was still achieving results as part of the process of hunting former SS members.

Frank Foley finally retired to Stourbridge in 1949 and died there nine years later. But this son of Highbridge, named a 'British Hero of the Holocaust' by the British Government, is by no means forgotten, not in his hometown, or in the annals of the Jewish nation.

J

ILCHESTER GAOL

Prison conditions in the eighteenth and nineteenth centuries were not that unreasonable if the various books of regulations were to be believed, but the reality was vastly different. Bath was the only Somerset gaol with a good reputation. In the earlier years, those at Shepton Mallet, Taunton and Bridgwater were badly run and the one at Ilchester was the worst of the lot. That town had provided the county's main penal accommodation for nearly 700 years with the first prison (*c.*1166–1429) on a site off the High Street, the second (1429–1620) located on the bridge over the River Ivel, and the third (1620–1843) on the north bank of the river.

The notorious former gaol at Ilchester stood on the site behind this wall along the River Ivel.

In February 1779 the county gaol at Ilchester had forty-eight prisoners, which was more than the other four main Somerset gaols put together. All but one of the prisoners were males, and no less than thirty-two were debtors. The prison was modified several times and its capacity increased to sixty-seven single cells, but in the first part of the nineteenth century the typical inmate population rose steadily from around 150 to over 200, and eventually even more. By the 1820s the proportion of debtors had dropped to 26 per cent, and nearly half of the inmates were classed as felons (the remainder serving shorter sentences for minor misdemeanours). Around this time, the definition of a felony was the involvement of goods worth more than 1*s*. This was exactly the same sum as was being charged for access to a coal wharf on the opposite side of the river to view an execution!

'The Rules and Regulations for the Government of the Common Gaol and House of Correction' at Ilchester in 1821 laid down quite comprehensive instructions about the management of the prison. To see that they were carried out, a Master was appointed and had to deposit a bond for double his annual salary to secure his honest and effective services. The taskmaster had to provide a £500 surety and even the turnkeys had to provide a bond to the value of £200. The duties of each were clearly laid down, as were those of the matron, the chaplain and the surgeon and even the wardsmen, who acted as janitors. There were arrangements for scrutiny by 'visiting Justices' to see that everything was in order.

(From a Thomas Bewick woodcut)

But was it? There was little suggestion otherwise until the radical reformer Henry Hunt arrived to serve his two-and-a half year sentence for a disorder at Manchester and revealed the truth about Ilchester Gaol and the rule of the governor, William Bridle. Hunt's book *Investigation at Ilchester Gaol* exposed Bridle's despotic rule, in which those who could yield him money or other benefits were given incredible licence, and those who could not, or had offended him, received quite barbarous punishment. The latter would be condemned to suffer in one of nine solitary cells, with sixty-eight prisoners being so confined in 1823-24. Some prisoners were whipped, some put in irons, some 'blistered', and some even undergoing the near-forgotten torture of being 'pressed' with heavy weights.

The debtors in Ilchester's 'upper cells' – those who could support themselves – lived in reasonable comfort. The official regulations allowed them to send out for two pints of drink a day, and some of this was undoubtedly consumed in the governor's quarters, where drinking and gambling were commonplace and provided William Bridle with a substantial illicit income. The prison accounts, labour records and day book showed none of this, nor anything of the illicit earnings siphoned off from the prisoners' labour and prison supply contracts.

An investigation prompted by the appearance of Hunt's allegations brought an end to Bridle's regime, but he even had the nerve to reapply for his old post when it was advertised again in 1838. Mismanagement and abuse aside, Ilchester was a substandard gaol, prone to typhoid and gaol fever because of its low, waterside location. It was frequently overcrowded, and by 1842, when the 'silent system' was introduced into prisons, was clearly unfit for purpose. On 1 March of the following year Wilton became the county gaol and the Ilchester premises were emptied, advertised and eventually sold.

J

JACK WHITE'S CONFESSION

One description of the terrible crime of Jack White of Wincanton in 1730 describes his attack on one Robert Sutton in the stark phrase, 'He beat out one of his eyes, ran the stick in at his mouth and out through the neck, and otherwise mangled his victim.' It contrasts strongly with the sentiments which White expressed in the confession he made just before his execution. Granted he may well have been prompted, but nevertheless the words with which he concluded that confession do have a great poignancy. They were simply, 'I beg the World not to cast any Reflections on my Relations, on account of my shameful end; and particularly on my dear and innocent Wife, who has behav'd herself with great Tenderness to me, even in a common Gaol'.

The forty-year-old White had married Sarah Slade in 1716 and, although somewhat workshy and given to drink, seems to have led an unremarkable existence until one fateful day in the summer of 1730. That was the day that he met Robert Sutton, a stranger to the locality, who came into the Sun Inn where White was drinking and asked for directions to aid him in delivering a message he was carrying. As White recorded:

> … going along Wincanton, one Gilbert, at the Sign of the Sun, called me into his House, where I drank hard; when the Deceased came in, who was in Liquor, and offered me a Drink to go along with him, which I agreed to, and went with him out of Town, directing him in his Way, as well as I was able …

Apparently there had been some lively discussions in the Sun prior to the two leaving the inn and both men were pretty drunk as they headed out of Wincanton on the Castle Cary road. It was a hot day, and they had not got very far before coming to the conclusion that a short doze in the sun would refresh them and clear their heads. Although Sutton recovered himself sufficiently to remember the message he was carrying and resume his journey, he soon lost his way and had to come back to seek White's guidance once more. The two again set off together. But, as Jack records:

> … in our Way we met two Women, one of whom I saluted, but the other being stubborn, provoked me to strike her, and as far as my Memory can retain, the Deceased and I had Words about them, and also would force me to go along with him to his Journey's End; taking a Counter out of his Pocket, cursing and swearing that it was half a guinea, and that he would spend it all upon me …

Reading between the lines of the confession, it seems that the whole mood of the situation had now changed. Jack White had not taken kindly to the rejection of his amorous advances towards the second girl and even less to having the error of his ways pointed out to him by a stranger. Resentment and the lure of possible cash led him to a point where, 'through Drunkenness and the Devil's Suggestion', he wrenched a stake from the hedgerow and made the frenzied attack upon Robert Sutton described earlier.

Unable to conceal the murder he had committed, White was quickly arrested and taken to Ilchester Gaol. His trial at the Bridgwater Assizes on 6 August 1730 inevitably led to a conviction and the death sentence. The murderer was hanged thirteen days later at the site of his crime, where the Wincanton–Castle Cary road is crossed by the one from Holton to Bratton Seymour. His body was then encased in a gibbet to remain as terrible evidence of the fate accorded to murderers.

K

KERSEYS, PENISTONES AND SAGATHEES

For over four centuries wool and woollen cloth were of major importance in the Somerset economy, with individual centres specialising in their own materials and markets. At its height, the wool and cloth business was the vital mainstay of commerce and wealth in Somerset, with many a fine church and clothier's house still bearing witness to the industry and subsequent generosity of those who made their fortunes from it. Countless sheep grazed the lush, green landscape and their wool, originally a major export, was processed wherever water was available for power and cleansing and a sufficient labour force could be found to carry out the dozen or so processes involved in turning the fleeces into finished cloth.

The Frome area, Wells and Shepton Mallet were producing substantial quantities of broadcloth before the end of the fourteenth century. Cloth production then grew steadily, based on a pattern of the initial processes being carried out in small farm and cottage units, until the cloth was taken to fulling mills for thickening. From centres in the east of the county, much of the output went to Lyme Regis for export, while from western areas it would be shipped at Exeter or Topsham, or sometimes Bridgwater or Minehead. Another distinction was the tendency for the west of the county to concentrate on the lighter serges, and the east to mix in imported wool to make the so-called Spanish medleys. Whatever the speciality, yards in the major producing areas like Taunton, Wellington, Shepton Mallet and Frome would be places of constant activity, full of baled cloth for loading onto lumbering wagons or onto the backs of a string of pack horses, led and guided by a knowing bell-horse.

The original fleece would determine the length of the woollen strands and the degrees of fineness or coarseness of the thread. The cleaning and dyeing processes would not vary greatly, but the choice of thread and weave would determine which of a number of different cloths were produced. Individual areas, mills and manufacturers tended to have their own specialities, resulting in a variety of names for their own particular cloth. In some cases these took the name of the place of their manufacture. On offer were 'Tauntons', 'Bridgwaters' and 'Bath Beavers', for example.

(From a Thomas Bewick woodcut)

Some names are still familiar to us. Serge, for example, is a durable twilled worsted fabric. Its constituent, worsted, uses long and coarse wool, which would have been combed in the longitudinal warp and softer, shorter, carded wool for the weft. The coarser wools were plentiful in Somerset, and their use as kerseys was a speciality of the Flemish weavers who settled in the county. Dunster produced the finer kerseymeres and Taunton 'sagathees' and 'duroys', the former a mixture of serge and silk which was used in better-class clothing for gentlemen.

One of Wiveliscombe's specialities was 'penistones', a thick, rubbed cloth which went to the West Indies. Dyed blue and stretched on the fields around the town, it met the slaves' entitlement to six yards of cloth every Christmas, but had a reputation for shrinking badly when wet, probably due to being overstretched in pursuit of profit. Prior to emancipation, its production was the main industry of the town, with the wool spun in local homes, sold at market and then woven in the town mills before being moved by pack horse or donkey to the Tone fulling mills. It returned after scouring and cleaning, to be dyed, washed and hung on the stretching racks before the final napping process.

Chard produced coarse cloth and cottons, and along with Frome and Ilminster, had a specific market in the provision of cloth used for liveries. Cary cloth was more suited to the uses of country folk, while blanketing came from Dulverton, Wellington and Wiveliscombe. Linsey woolseys were supplied by Milborne Port. Crewkerne was not only noted for its sailcloth,

This former mill at Chard is one of a number of fine examples surviving in Somerset. When the wool industry deserted Chard, the town became a centre for lace making with some 1,500 employed in the manufacture of plain lace.

but also supplied the East India Company with serges. With British interests all over the world and conflicts frequent, there was a strong and ongoing demand for uniform material; heavy and coarse for ordinary ranks, and of a better quality for officers.

The traditional woollen industry began to decline in the second half of the eighteenth century, the heart of the business passing to the increasingly mechanised mills of Yorkshire. American cotton and better transport were other factors, as was the sometimes violent resistance to new machinery in Somerset, especially in Shepton Mallet. Where machinery was installed in the nineteenth century woollen cloth continued to be important, but elsewhere its place was filled for a while by silk, a trade which had moved away from East London in 1773.

KEWSTOKE RELIC

Below Worlebury Hill, beyond the busy seafront at Weston-super-Mare, lies the small village of Kewstoke. Its irregular spread of older and modern houses and not a few holiday chalets and caravans sits placidly between the tree-covered hillside and the long stretch of sand that flanks Sand Bay. At the foot of the hill, where a steep road and a set of steps known as Monk's Steps both complete their descent,

Kewstoke parish church with Sand Bay and the Bristol Channel beyond.

lies the charming fifteenth-century Church of St Paul. For a long time its religious companion, a couple of miles along the coast, was Woodspring Priory. The two are linked by a drama that took place on the national scene many years ago and many miles away.

In 1170, just four days after Christmas, four noblemen forced their way into Canterbury Cathedral and brutally murdered its archbishop, Thomas Becket. The fifty-two-year-old Becket had been a talented young man who had come to the notice of Henry II. Becket had risen from minor duties to be the king's chancellor, and then to the archbishopric by the king's recognition of those talents. No doubt Henry expected total loyalty in return for the preferment, but the relationship proved turbulent when Becket insisted on resisting the frequent royal encroachment on the Church's affairs.

Famously supposed to have remarked in anger, 'Who will rid me of this turbulent priest,' Henry's flash of temper was interpreted by four of his noblemen as something which could be used to earn them royal favour. On the day of their shame, the four knights forced their way into Canterbury Cathedral at the time of vespers and demanded that Becket should absolve a number of men he had excommunicated and return those he had suspended to their various offices. A refusal led to exchanges that became more and more threatening, until one of the knights swung his sword at the archbishop's head and then severed the arm which a companion had raised to protect his spiritual master.

The assembled monks and clerics fled as the other assassins joined in, forcing Becket to his knees and cutting open his skull until the floor beside the altar was stained with blood.

That blood, spilled in Canterbury Cathedral in the twelfth century, forms the link between the two religious houses flanking Sand Bay in North Somerset. One of them, Woodspring Priory, was founded as a direct consequence of Becket's murder. Of the four cathedral killers – Sir Reginald Fitz Urse, Richard de Bret, William de Traci and Hugh de Morville – two had roots in Somerset; Fitz Urse at Williton and de Brett at Sampford Brett. Some land and property at Woodspring, or Worspring as it was then, also belonged to Fitz Urse and later passed via the marriage of his daughter to the de Courtenays. The four murderers had fled to Rome to seek papal absolution and had been condemned to permanent penance in Jerusalem, but the contrition of their families was ongoing and led to the foundation in 1210 of a small priory of the Augustinian order at Woodspring. It was an act of expiation, dedicated to the Virgin and to St Thomas.

The link with the Church of St Paul at Kewstoke derives from the act of another King Henry: Henry VIII's split with the Church of Rome and his removal of its power in the country. In the nationwide process of the Dissolution of the Monasteries, Woodspring, albeit a tiny establishment valued at only £87, did not escape and suffered the fate of so many other religious houses in 1536. The few remaining monks were treated well enough and the former prior, Richard Springe, received accommodation, servants, provisions, a supply of ale and his own privy. Significantly, the priory had earlier seen the writing on the wall and determined that one of its most precious possessions should not fall into secular hands.

The scene now moves to St Paul's church, where the weight of the clerestory was proving too much for one of the walls of the nave, forcing repairs to be carried out in 1849. This proved a major undertaking, involving partial demolition of the original masonry. In the process, a sculptured figure had to be removed, exposing a hitherto unsuspected niche. Inside, on a rounded base, a worn carved figure nestled between arches formed in the Early English style, with the whole modest piece topped by a conventional arch. Behind, and smaller still, was an arch within the arch which held a simple wooden cup, exceptional only for its obvious age and the dark stains inside its ancient bowl.

The tests carried out on the find clearly showed the stain to be that of human blood and expert opinion came to the conclusion that this was, in all probability, one of several relics emanating from the cathedral at Canterbury claiming to be samples of the blood of its murdered archbishop. The venerable relic unearthed at Kewstoke was passed to Taunton Museum by the Somerset Archaeological Society for safe keeping.

KING'S EVIL

Scrofula, a painful and often fatal disease of the lymphatic glands, was commonly known as the King's Evil. For centuries it defied the varied treatments of the medical men of the day, but there was a widespread belief that scrofula could be cured by the touch of a monarch. Right from the days of Edward the Confessor, successive kings had given credence to this belief by providing formal 'touching' sessions and requiring payment for doing so. Quite a number of these touchings took place in Bath, Bristol and Somerset.

The practice of touching reached extraordinary heights in the seventeenth century when King Charles II is reputed to have touched thousands. It was a weekly event attended by well-orchestrated proceedings which involved prior approval of suppliants by the royal surgeons, admission to the royal presence and then kneeling to the accompaniment of chanting and prayers. The king would pass a hand over the sufferer's swollen areas and say, 'May God heal thee'. Finally, a ribbon with a gold angel hanging from it would be placed around the patient's neck. This was to be worn until they were cured.

An extraordinary example of Somerset touching is recorded in a pamphlet which states:

> We, Henry Clark, Minister of the Parish of Crewkerne, Captain James Bale, Captain Richard Sherlock, John Stacky, clerk, &c., do certify the truth of the Miraculous Cure of a Girl of this Town, about 20 years ago, by name of Elizabeth Parcet, a poor widow's daughter, who hath languished under the sad afflicted distemper of the King's Evil, termed the Joint Evil, being held to be the worst Evil, for about Ten or Eleven years' time.
>
> Her Mother, not being of the ability to send her to London, to be touched by the King being miserable Poor, having many small children, and this girl not being able to work, her Mother sought to the Chirurgeons for help, who tampered with it for a time, but could do no good, went likewise 10 or 11 miles to a seventh son but all in vain.

SCROFULA

scrofula (skrof'ūlə), *n.* tuberculous condition, *espec.* of children, with enlargement of lymphatic glands of neck; king's evil. -lism, -losis, *n.* -litic, -lous, *adj.*

> Now the Duke of Monmouth, lying at Mr Speaks at Lackington, the Girl did often persuade her mother that she might go to Lackington, but certainly, said she, I should be well if I could but touch him.
>
> A few days after the Girl having notice that Sir John Sydenham intended to treat the Duke at White Lodge, in Henton Park, this Girl with many of her neighbours went to the same park, and as he was coming out she caught him by the bare handwrist with her hand saying, 'God bless your Greatness' and the Duke said, 'God bless you.'
>
> She came home to her Mother with great joy, and told her she should now be well and, to the admiration of all that know of it, her six wounds were dried up in four or five days; her eye that was given up for lost is now perfectly well, and the Girl is in good health.
>
> The marks of several wounds are yet visible in her hand and arm, all of which has been discovered to us both by Mother and Daughter and neighbours that know her.
>
> Whoever doubts the truth of this relation may be satisfied thereof by sight of the Original at the Amsterdam Coffee House in Bartholomew-lane, near the Royal Exchange.

Although his touching may have helped Elizabeth Parcet, it did no good for the Duke of Monmouth himself. Along with several other cases, it was brought up at his trial as part of a formal indictment of 'having touched children for the Evil'.

There were straightforward royal touchings of sufferers from Curry Rivel and Ling, and an unusual variant at Prestleigh in 1637. There, one William Gilbert let it be known that his five-year-old-son Richard, a survivor of seven born to William's wife, could effect cures by touching. This was in line with the common belief that the seventh son had this special power. He offered the examples of John Norton, an Evercreech weaver, and Rebecca Poynting, a young girl of East Pennard, as proof. Soon the Gilberts were running a regular Monday surgery and touching thirty or more patients a week. They were quite formal events with prayer and fasting and the actual touching accompanied by the benediction 'I touch and God heals'. However, this nice lucrative practice, which usurped the monarch's prerogative, could not fail to attract attention and eventually prompted an investigation by the bishop, who quickly 'did straightly charge and command' that it be stopped.

L

LITTLETON GUNPOWDER

On the Winford Brook, just east of Winford village and tucked away off the main road to Chew Magna, stands an imposing sixteenth-century house which once had its own tower and chapel and would not normally be taken for a former factory. However for many years, the house and its adjoining buildings operated as a gunpowder mill, using the water power of the brook to turn saltpetre, charcoal and sulphur into the powder essential for guns and blasting operations, and using a manufacturing process that was quite complex and not a little hazardous to do so.

The manufacture of gunpowder in quantity appears to stem from the availability of increased supplies of saltpetre brought from India by the East India Co. in the seventeenth century. The process was normally located in a fairly remote spot not too far from a port, and the establishment of a gunpowder mill at Woolley, north of Bath, in 1722 is probably connected with the expansion of Bristol's port activity resulting from the slave trade. The manufacture of powder began at Littleton some twenty years later and there was at least one further Somerset mill at work, located at Moreton, now beneath the waters of Chew Valley Lake.

By the 1750s the Littleton activity was owned and operated by five leading Bristol merchants. One of them, Jeremiah Ames, appears to have been the leading light. The previous military market clearly fluctuated with the extent of the country's conflicts, but this link with commercial men gave the business important access to the shipping activity of the city. In addition to the requirements of the many privateer vessels and of modestly armed merchant ships, there was a great demand for gunpowder in Africa and America; most slaving vessels carried an appreciable amount. When the *Dispatch* sailed on a voyage to purchase 240 slaves in 1725 it carried as part of its cargo 180 'musquets' and ten barrels of gunpowder worth over £40.

For seventeen years from 1751, William Dyer was the accountant for the Littleton Mill gunpowder enterprise and recorded something of its life during that period. One of the constantly recurring issues in that account is the problem of finding suitable storage for this highly dangerous commodity.

For many years the warehouse for gunpowder in Bristol was the Tower Harritz, which stood on a site now occupied by Temple Meads railway station. It supplied all the privateers and merchant vessels sailing from the port. However, in 1745 the local magistrates became apprehensive about the quantity of explosive stored there and the risk it represented, and ordered its removal to Portishead Creek. Clearly this did not happen, for in 1751 the Littleton partner Jeremiah Ames had

Main and outbuildings of the former gunpowder factory at Littleton Mill.

acquired a property at Hung Road and, 'apprehensive of a search being made at Tower Harritz', was desperately looking for a gunpowder magazine site near his new purchase. In the meantime, some powder had to be quickly moved from the tower by river wherry, and the loading and unloading of shipping gunpowder was increasingly carried out at a downriver store.

The process of making the gunpowder at Littleton involved refining the saltpetre, which had to be boiled, drained, washed and crystallised. The sulphur and charcoal ingredients – in 1753 dogwood charcoal was carted in from Guildford – were each boiled and sieved. Using horse power plus the waters of the brook built up in a long millpond, these ingredients were mixed in a pestle mill and then moistened, glazed, pressed and heat dried. In the early days the drying process used an open heat source, which did not help the accident record. The gunpowder end product was packed in 100lb barrels made by a Bristol firm of coopers.

In addition to the main house at Littleton, a barn on the left was used for storage and a block to the right accommodated the mill workmen, 'a small number' in 1751. Other buildings housed the main processes, but a severe fire in November 1755 destroyed 'the charge room, petre store, charcoal loft and horse mill'. A bell in the clock tower was used as a warning when powder was being moved, but the whole activity was extremely dangerous and mishaps were not infrequent. There was also a fire at the Tower Harritz itself in the following year. Once the damage there had been made good, 200 French prisoners were moved in, resulting in more problems for Littleton, as it had to find somewhere else for the stock of brimstone it kept at the tower.

The markets for gunpowder were mainly military, for ships and for 'shops', the latter presumably referring to such private uses as hunting, blasting and so on. Littleton's 'shops' production was sent to a stable on Redcliff Back in October 1756 for storage, but so many local people objected that the mayor ordered it back to Tower Harritz. The gunpowder mill at Woolley sold mainly to the 'shops' and did little business with the Bristol ship merchants. This was the Littleton strength, along with the fact that its owners rented a room in the Exchange Coffee House and ran the Gunpowder Office from there so as to be close to prospective purchasers.

Unlike the Woolley factory, Littleton was always short of storage space and the two companies came near to establishing a partial amalgamation based on combining their sales activity and storage arrangements, but keeping the production separate. Nothing came of this and the gunpowder making at Littleton continued to be hindered by this lack of space. In 1758 the company had to withdraw its gunpowder work from a former fulling mill nearby when the rent was increased. Three years later, it was unable to carry out a contract with the Board of Ordnance for 1,000 barrels of gunpowder at 87*s* a barrel.

By 1764 the firm was expressing interest in converting a one-time snuff mill at Stanton Drew to gunpowder production. By this time, production had reached around 3,500 barrels a year.

William Dyer became a shareholder in the Littleton enterprise in 1763, using money advanced by the existing partners. It seems that in return he was virtually required to run the place and even moved there for a time. After five years he relinquished his one-eighth share, returned the advance and handed over control to his brother Robert. In 1776 Jeremiah Ames died, a very rich man.

The transport of gunpowder produced at Woolley was undertaken in wagons using leather sheets to protect the load. Littleton probably did the same, but the remains of a wooden punt were recovered there some time after the mill ceased operation and may have been used for local movements along minor streams. Most of the Littleton output went to Bristol, but the mill probably also produced blasting powder for use in local mines and quarries.

Less information is available about the years after William Dyer severed his connection with the Litleton mill, but gunpowder production continued there until around 1820. It had peaked during the Napoleonic Wars, but the huge subsequent decline in the military market, coupled with the end of slavery in 1807 and America building up its own gunpowder production, reduced demand to such an extent that the industry was no longer viable. Later in the century the location is recorded just as Powder Mill Farm, its 'long millpond' having long been emptied.

LIGHTHOUSE BONANZA

In times of poor visibility and before modern aids became available, the small boats operating into and out of Somerset harbours needed all the navigational help they could get. In some cases, hilltop beacons were lit. In others the seaward tower of a church in an elevated position would be coated with whitewash to provide guidance, thanks to the incumbent's goodwill and a donation from the local community's seafarers. At Burnham, a woman from the small fishing fraternity was paid a small sum for exhibiting a lighted lantern when the menfolk needed it.

As seaborne trade increased, these limited navigational aids were clearly less than adequate and were, in some coastal areas, displaced by simple lighthouses built by some local entrepreneur in anticipation of recouping the cost from a small payment by ship masters. Such was the case on the island of Flat Holm, a strategic remnant of the end of the Mendip Hills, lying midway between the English and Welsh shores of the Bristol Channel. All vessels heading for or setting out from Bristol or the lower waters of the Severn Estuary passed this islet.

The lessee of Flat Holm put forward a proposal for a lighthouse there in 1736. A terrible Channel shipwreck the following year, in which sixty soldiers lost their lives gave great impetus to the scheme, and by the December of that year the island's new lighthouse was in operation. It had ruined its original builders owing to onerous conditions imposed by the Bristol Society of Merchant Venturers, but when completed, earned tolls of 3*d* a ton on all foreign shipping and half that figure on the cargoes of all Bristol ships.

The lighthouse concept itself dates back at least to Roman times and the Corporation of Trinity House had been granted its first royal charter in 1514, but contented itself with licensing private lighthouses and collecting handsome fees for doing so. By the beginning of the nineteenth century it was in need of reform and this came about in legislation of 1822 which included provisions for Trinity House to purchase outright the lease of existing private lighthouses. The Corporation took over the Flat Holm light in the following year and paid out £15,838 for the privilege, based upon a commutation of the tolls for the remaining duration of the lease.

Back in Burnham, a Welsh clergyman had arrived in the tiny fishing village in 1791 and taken up residence in the vicarage behind the sand dunes. It was not unusual for clergymen to have interests beyond their prime calling and the Revd David Davies was no exception. Often these interests were associated with the arts or one of the branches of science, but those without a private income had to think in more practical terms if their stipend and tithes were

Beyond the churchyard at Burnham-on-Sea stands the castelated stump of the first of the town's three lighthouses.

only modest. Whatever the motivation, the new curate displaced the lady with the lantern by providing a light from the tower of his church, duly collecting the fees for this service.

The number of vessels passing along the River Parrett between Bridgwater and the awkward approach waters between Burnham and Steart Point steadily increased over the years. This, coupled with the bishop's reservations about his use of the church tower, led Davies to build his own light tower in a prominent position where the dunes met the churchyard. It seems likely that Davies was not dependent on his stipend or the lighthouse tolls for capital, as he began to acquire land in the area, and then set in motion drilling for local springs. He lived at a time when there was much faith in the healing powers of mineral waters, and his second drilling venture located waters of chalybeate saline with a sulphur content at a depth of 25ft.

Given Trinity House approval in 1815, the Davies lighthouse was acquired by that body fourteen years later for the sum of £13,681. David Davies himself had been given a fresh appointment in Hampshire in 1813, but retained his interest in Burnham, and with considerable capital now available, could pursue his plan for a development to service the growing interest in spas and health-giving sea locations. At the same time, this would both provide local employment and represent a good use of his money. The centrepiece was

Although located on the seafront at Burnham, Steart House was built facing inland and the original frontage overlooked an area of gardens, part of the 'Daviesville' development.

Steart House, a tall seafront building providing spa facilities and accommodation, and still to be seen today, albeit now apartments. More residential and visitor accommodation was built along either side, with a large area behind devoted to 'Pleasure Grounds'.

Davies' spa building had baths on the lower floor providing four different temperatures, with seawater immersion also available, along with sea bathing, special diets and other features. Above were reception, library and meeting rooms, plus accommodation for staying guests. This enterprising cleric died before the whole of his dream development was completed, and the spa itself declined in the 1860s with the general drop in the fashion, but Steart House and its companion buildings on the seafront at Burnham-on-Sea still bear witness to this Welshman's vision.

LOST HARBOUR

The level coastal plain between the Quantock Hills and the Bristol Channel is a quiet, pleasant area, much of it once part of the vast estates of notable landowners. Amongst these was the Acland family, whose home was at Fairfield House, a short way along the old road from Stogursey to Kilve. Between Stert

The grassy hollow between the shingle beach and the overgrown masonry was once the enclosed dock at Lilstock.

Flats and Watchet the coastline of this area is a succession of low cliffs, shingle foreshore and a black rock bottom. The odd small stream flows into the Bristol Channel and one of these, a modest affair, provides a signpost to the site of a former harbour, largely forgotten for over a century, but once a busy place serving the Acland estates.

Lilstock's limekilns were located between the footbridge over the dock entrance and the buildings along the quay beyond.

The mouth of the stream had been used from time to time by small sailing vessels bringing coal over from the expanding pits of South Wales to fuel the estate fires and limekilns. Wood from the estate was turned into pit props to provide the occasional return load. In the 1830s Sir John Acland, intent on the improvement of his landholdings, turned this casual shipping activity into something vastly more significant.

Sir John's granddaughter, Isabel, was in poor health at the time and the benefits of sea air were prescribed for her treatment. To provide this, a small wooden house overlooking the sea was built for her on the high ground east of the stream, and a promenade created along the shoreline below. At the same period, a long dock was excavated behind the promenade and lined with masonry; the stream was diverted to help maintain its water level. Entrance gates and sluices were provided at the other end to create a substantial harbour capable of holding several vessels which could now discharge their cargoes of coal and limestone, independent of the tides and sheltered from bad weather.

The activity at Lilstock Harbour increased steadily and by 1844 warranted the appointment of a resident coastguard. A customs officer followed in 1855 and the harbour approaches were later improved by the building of a protective stone pier out from the entrance. What had started as a beaching place had become a useful working harbour and, in parallel, the social activity had grown steadily so as to now warrant the provision of a 'butler's pantry' at the end of the new pier to facilitate picnics for the visitors arriving in their horse-drawn coaches. Additionally, a simple warehouse behind the dock proved useful for the social events of Lilstock village.

Lilstock village itself expanded, and a coastguard's cottage and two more substantial houses were constructed along the walled quay beyond the harbour entrance. Nearby were two large limekilns built into the face of the cliff behind, fired by coal brought into the dock and providing fertiliser for the estate farms.

Lilstock also featured in one of the several schemes to provide a ship canal from the Bristol Channel to South Devon.

The trows and ketches using Lilstock Harbour were, for a while, joined by steamers landing or picking up excursionists at the quay. They could visit the pub there or stroll along the foreshore; and a tearoom facility existed right up until the early years of the twentieth century. The area thrived until a brutal storm hit, which caused serious damage to the harbour and its surrounds. Trade was declining, the general pattern of life was changing and there was an ongoing problem with shingle encroachment. By the end of the First World War, Lilstock Harbour was completely abandoned and all evidence of the activity there slowly disappeared over the years that followed, until only a grass-covered hollow, odd portions of masonry and two bramble-enshrouded limekilns were left to mark the spot.

M

MARKET DAY MAYHEM

WIVELISCOMBE 1605

Today Wiveliscombe is a small, quiet town where it is difficult to imagine the most extraordinary events which appear to have taken place there on market day on 9 July 1605 and again just a week later. The principal character in these dramas was one William Cappes, or Capps, described as a gentleman, but apparently anything but gentle in his behaviour. The leading opposition characters were bailiff Henry Washer and tithingman Joseph Yea.

The subsequent enquiry into the events implied that when confronted by the two officers, Cappes not only insulted them and the law they represented, but also went completely berserk. Suspecting that Washer and Yea held warrants

The Square at Wiveliscombe.

demanding his good behaviour, Cappes apparently said to Washer, 'Stand further from me, I cannot abide thy breath', and then promptly set upon the pair. Cappes was also accused of wandering up and down the market 'in a most distracted state' with no shirt or hat and with his 'hanger or rapier drawn in a furious manner', causing the market day throng to be 'much afrighted and amazed.'

Further questioning of the witnesses suggested that matters were even worse on the next market day when Cappes came to town dressed in 'a privy coat and shirt of mail' and was accused of throwing his hanger (sword) at John Yea, fully intending to kill him. The rampaging then continued, with Cappes breaking into the house of innkeeper John Hobbs, knocking him down and then trying to wound David, another Yea, by poking his rapier through a window. When the local Justice of the Peace was summoned, he read the Riot Act and instructed Cappes and his supporters to drop their weapons and leave, but his peacemaking efforts received nothing but defiance.

Nor did the matter end there for just five days later, on the Sunday, Cappes and John Yea met again on a road just outside the town. Still smarting from the earlier events, the angry 'gentleman' was soon waving his rapier again, and poor John Yea was so frightened that he fell off his horse and took to his heels.

When presented at the enquiry into these matters on 30 November 1605, the case against William Cappes looked extremely serious. He did not deny his aggressive behaviour, but revealed that there were other things which ought to be taken into account. According to Cappes, the events of the first market day all started with a man named Jenkins badly wounding another named Amyas Towt. John Cappes, William's brother, promptly joined him in chasing Jenkins, whom they apprehended and relieved of two daggers. William then conveyed the wounded man to the house of Widow Taylor for attention. Far from running berserk around the town, William averred he was actually hurrying to fetch a doctor for Towt, still carrying a confiscated sword, and shirtless because he had used it to stop the injured man's bleeding. When he saw Washer armed with a staff, previous bad blood between them made him suspicious of his motives; hence the threats with the sword.

When Cappes had first given his version of the events on 16 July it became clear that the two sides had a history of antagonism. He stated that John Yea had walked past him several times carrying a corn pike, giving him 'ill words'. Cappes, not a man to be trifled with, reacted after being 'first hurted' by Yea and promptly threw his hanger at him, only to be knocked down by one of his cronies. The wounded Cappes managed to stagger to Widow Taylor's house, where he armed himself with one of the weapons from the earlier assault on Towt and set off for Hobbs' inn and the abortive attempt to stab Yea through one of the windows. He then wounded one of Yea's cronies in the shoulder before rejoining his own supporters.

When it came to the encounter on the following Sunday, Cappes stated that he had been on his way to have his wounds dressed by a surgeon and admitted that when he met John Yea he 'meant to have hurt him.' He had heard nothing, he said, of a market day declaration by a Justice of the Peace calling for order, for he had already left town. With no other information being forthcoming, we can only speculate on what followed.

NETHER STOWEY 1608

Equally bizarre, but no better resolved, was the situation at Nether Stowey three years after the Wiveliscombe affair. The central character was a merchant named Edmund Whetcombe of whom it was said at an enquiry into the whole matter: 'local brute and fame in and about the borrowe of Nether Stowey was that Whetcombe had secretly purloined and stolen out of the grounds of Andrew Prowse one grey gelding, and that he did closely keep the same gelding in his stable with the doors locked.'

It seems that Andrew Prowse was so convinced of Whetcombe's guilt that he sought and obtained a search warrant from Sir Nicholas Halswell, Justice of the Peace, which was duly presented by two constables and a bailiff. All they got for their pains were 'ill and indecent speeches', so they left empty-handed. Whetcombe offered a different version of the visit, alleging that a disorderly crowd surrounded his home late at night armed with 'Bills, Clubs, Swords, Daggers and Long Staves' and besieged the place until daybreak.

The local ill-feeling towards Whetcombe found curious expression in the market place at Nether Stowey on 7 April 1608. Out of the blue, two strangers appeared, and after getting the attention of the crowd with the customary Oyez, they proclaimed: 'All manner of persons that have any old shreds of leather, old ropes, old clouts, or any old boots or shoes, let them repair to Edmond Whetcombe, and they shall have utterance for their wares.'

Reading between the lines of the witness statements, this extraordinary event was all part of a well-orchestrated campaign against Whetcombe. The reason appears to have been that he was too pretentious for the people of Nether Stowey, and this unsought delivery of worn-out materials was one of the elements in a concerted plan to deflate his ego.

More of the background story unfolded with the evidence of local weaver Edward Davie. He revealed that some time earlier he had been brought an ancient paper by Richard Calverwell, which turned out to be a royal document authorising the Whetcombes to trade in 'the gatherance of all manner of linen rags.' Despite his self-described status as a merchant, with its implied respectability, here was evidence that Edmund Whetcombe was little more than a rag-and-bone man. As part of the ongoing campaign against his perceived vanity, his enemies had also sent Whetcombe a package containing four cards, all depicting knaves, and a message reading, 'Be not offended because thou hast the style of Pedler, for it is well known that thy parentage was so.'

In the Nether Stowey case, the constables were criticised for doing nothing to halt the two hirelings who had made the market place proclamation. At Wiveliscombe the local law officers had clearly taken sides, both cases a reflection on local affairs at the beginning of the seventeenth century. They also prompt speculation on how seriously or otherwise perjury was taken at that time!

MENDIP MINING

The Mendip Hills were an important source of lead until the workings ran out and other sources of supply, notably Derbyshire, supplanted the local product. This upland area of Somerset also yielded a great deal of coal and stone from a number of quarries, but their extraction was mostly done by larger concerns, whereas the mining of lead and calamine was for many years a highly individual activity. Single miners, partners and mining families were licensed by the powerful landowners of the Middle Ages in return for a percentage of the yield.

The first known mining on Mendip was under the Romans when there is evidence of the extraction of lead by AD 49, just six years after their landing in Britain. An area at Charterhouse became a major centre of the activity with a small garrison nearby. Known as Verbriacum, it had roads leading south west for the lead pigs destined for Rome and the Empire, north east through the Chew Valley for the Avon, and to the Bristol Channel.

Lead mining continued on Mendip through the post-Roman era with mining rights in what was then a royal forest, being granted to the Bishop of Bath & Wells in the late twelfth century. By the 1500s the four Lords Royal of Mendip – the Bishop plus the lordships of East Harptree, Chewton Mendip and Charterhouse – had organised the mining area into four 'liberties' with a clear system for the issue of licences to mine in return for 'lot lead' – 10 per cent of any ore produced.

From 1470 onwards, old agreements and practices had been crystallised into a set of mining laws by royal command. These remained in effect for many years, with control and change in the hands of mine courts, which met twice a year and had two jury levels. Implementation was in the hands of a Lead Reeve, who took an oath to carry out the orders of the court, report offences and collect the lot lead. Expanded over time to meet changing circumstances, the main provisions of these laws covered:

- Setting up: Anyone could seek a mining licence from the appropriate lordship and, if granted, could mine at will and forever, provided the laws were observed. Individual claims were made by the miner standing in his chosen pit up to the waist and then throwing his working tool as far as he could in any direction along a suspected vein of ore to mark the limit of his claim.
- Running: Good behaviour was required of all miners, with no weapons, fighting or disorder permitted. Increasingly, directives had to be imposed to meet the complaints of landowners that their cattle and pastures were being poisoned by inefficient washing of the lead. Stealing was loathed, but common, despite a stringent penalty that provided for theft to be dealt with in the following manner:

> If any man do steal any lead or ore to the value of thirteen
> pence halfpenny, the lord or his officer may arrest all his
> lead and ore ... with all his goods ... and put him in his
> house or work, and set everything on fire about him.

The search for lead-bearing deposits was mainly done by divining rod, with claims then explored and abandoned if they proved unfruitful. The early mining took place on or near the land surface, with the ore being smelted on an open hearth, draught-fed by primitive bellows, and the end product despatched by pack horse. Later, each liberty had its own washing places, or 'buddles', and smelting furnaces to facilitate the Lead Reeves' collection of the landlords' lot lead.

Around the middle of the seventeenth century lead production was at its peak, but then began to decline. Generally very narrow and pitted with breaks, the easy lodes nearest to the surface had been worked out and the search for new lodes around Charterhouse, Priddy and Shipham was increasingly forsaken due to other interests. Mining at greater depths improved the solution for a time, but many seams ran too deep for the technology of the age and the capacity to pump out water.

The next century saw the end of the old mining industry, but also the beginning of a revival at Charterhouse in 1824 based on the resmelting of the old refuse.

New methods could produce a worthwhile yield, owing to the limited efficiency of the older extraction. Around the middle of the century, the Mendip Mining Company brought in Cornish miners and mining practices, including reverberatory furnaces and the use of round buddles, comprising pits lined with masonry. The lead-laden fumes passed from furnaces via the buddles to long flues in which the lead was deposited, then to be scraped off after the smoke had been exhausted through tall chimneys. Until its end in the 1880s, much of the output went to Sheldon Bush's shot tower in Redcliffe Hill, Bristol.

The remains of lead flues at Charterhouse.

Mining for lead was a hard life involving tough physical labour. As shafts sank deeper, workings became more cramped and precarious and more liable to inundation by water or rock falls. On the surface, the washing, smelting and casting of the ore was equally onerous. The rewards were unpredictable, for seams varied and markets had their peaks and troughs, but the working costs remained. Tools, timber, troughs, chutes and simple moving and lifting equipment all had to be provided, whatever ore was produced. Inhaling the lead fumes resulted in ill health which, in turn, might lead to neglect of a claim and its forfeiture. But, despite all this, the sense of community saw miners commit themselves to recovering and burying the body of any miner lost below ground, however deep down it might be.

Some lead was mined in the Shipham area, but the miners there and at Rowberrow specialised in the extraction of calamine for use in the manufacture of brass, sometimes coming across the thin zinc ore-bearing veins in shafts sunk to mine lead. The calamine mining functioned in much the same way as in the lead liberties, and peaked in the eighteenth century, when a great deal of the output went to the brass mill at Saltford. The calamine produced was of good quality and when carefully calcined could fetch up to £7 a ton.

In the Shipham area it became commonplace for miners to unite their living quarters and their mining activity on the same plot. Moralists and reformers viewed their general behaviour with disfavour, but life was hard and times were different then. Some extraction continued until the 1870s, but most of the workings had been abandoned some twenty years earlier, and their miners had sought temporary relief from poverty by applying for jobs with the Mendip Mining Company at Charterhouse.

MINEHEAD TRAGEDY

Sailings between Bristol and Ireland were commonplace and had been taking place for centuries. There would have been few apprehensions on this score in Bristol at 8 a.m., Friday, 20 February 1736 as two regiments of troops marched to join the vessels that were to take them to their posting across the Irish Sea. With drums beating, families and baggage following behind and a few early risers to cheer them on their way, the expectation was of a safe arrival in Ireland the same evening. But that was not to be.

The fleet of transport vessels sailed out into the Bristol Channel in good conditions but then ran into a dramatic change of weather. In Bridgwater Bay they encountered blinding sleet followed by heavy snow which reduced visibility to near zero, scattering the ships in all directions. One of them, the *Lamb*, totally lost its way with the tragic consequences later reported by *Read's Weekly Journal*:

> On Wednesday came the melancholy news that the Lamb, Captain Morgan, from Bristol to Waterford, with one company complete and part of another, of Colonel Hargreave's regiment, ordered to return to Ireland, was cast away on Saturday last (Feb. 21st) upon Minehead strand. Captain Frankford and Captain Williamson, belonging to the said regiment, had the misfortune to perish, as did 76 other persons, part of whom were the soldiers' wives and children; the sailors and 40 passengers were saved by getting on the shrouds. Most of the dead bodies drove on the shore the same day.

Exactly what happened to the *Lamb* in that blinding storm is a matter for conjecture, but the fact that a third of its complement survived by clinging to the rigging provides a clue. A likely scenario is that, with no chance of fixing its position, the ship was driven off its course and impaled itself on an offshore rock outcrop at a time when the tide was ebbing, and that those who could not climb above deck level were swept away when it turned and flooded back. With everything shrouded in snow and sleet there would have been no hope of being sure what was happening either on board or on shore, and no rescue attempt could be mounted.

Whatever the exact cause, the parish records of Minehead and Dunster bear sombre witness to the tragedy, for they detail the burial of thirty-five bodies in Minehead churchyard on one day and another seven subsequently. The Dunster register for 22 February notes, '19 soldiers, a boy, and two women and two children were buried which were drownded ye day before.'

⁂ MONUMENT TO BRAVERY

The coast of Somerset made its own special contribution to the Second World War. It provided pill boxes, tank obstacles, airfields and factories, practice bombing areas, secret weapon testing locations and, on the Pawlett Hams, a site for experiments in cutting the cables of tethered balloons. The Royal Aircraft Establishment chose this fairly isolated spot in 1940 to conduct experiments to find out whether it was feasible to provide aircraft with a method of cutting balloon cables. Success would provide a means of nullifying balloon defences, and a real prospect that an encounter between balloon and aircraft did not automatically result in a disaster for the latter. To house the balloons used in the tests a huge hangar was built, and a small unit of men to look after them was accommodated nearby.

The former balloon hanger at Pawlett, showing signs of its age.

The tests at Pawlett involved raising the balloon using the normal restraining cable plus a second one festooned with red warning flags. Various types of fighter and medium bomber aircraft fitted with cutting equipment had then deliberately to be flown into the flagged cable in an attempt to sever it. The risks were enormous and required a very special type of pilot to take them on. Sadly, several perished in the attempt. However, despite the ravages of time, the hangar was to linger on long after the hair-raising trials had ceased, to act as a rather unusual memorial to the bravery of the airmen involved.

N

NONSUCH NEAR HOME

Back in 1871 a book of limericks was published under the title *Sing a Song of Nonsense: A Book of Somerset Limericks*, and more verses have appeared from time to time. The selection below provides a mini-tour of the county:

There was a young lady of Barrow,
Whose mouth you couldn't call narrow!
She could swallow cucumbers
Quite whole, and in numbers
But choked when she tried a large marrow.

There was a young man of Bridgwater,
Who courted a chimney-sweep's daughter;
But so long he tarried,
That the young lady married,
A more soot-able soot-er who sought her.

There was an old lady of Brent
Whose nose was remarkably bent;
And the neighbours suppose
That she followed her nose,
For they cannot find which way she went.

There was a young lady of Cary,
At a fancy ball posed as a fairy
But of huge build and bone,
She weighed sixteen stone
And found dancing partners rather chary.

A jolly young farmer of Cheddar,
Was gone on a maiden and wed her;
But soon he found out
She couldn't do nowt,
So he sold off his farm and he fled her.

A lady of Chilton on Polden
Had locks most delightfully golden;
Some said, 'Nature's blessing,'
But others, just guessing
Were sure she to 'art' was beholden.

There was a young woman of Durston,
Who thought her third husband the worst 'un;
For he justly was reckoned
Far worse than the second,
And the second was worse than the first 'un.

There was an old farmer of Street,
Who prided himself on his wheat;
His barley was fine
His oats quite divine,
And his corns even covered his feet.

A dandy young fellow of Trull,
Once remarked that all women were dull;
But this so enraged
Ladies, both young and aged,
That he had to watch out for his skull.

There was an old woman of Wedmore,
Who said, 'There is nothing I dread more,
Than rising at five,
To be frozen alive,
So I think I shall stick to my bed more!'

There was an old fellow of Wellow,
Who played on the trombone and cello;
When neighbours protested,
He just laughed and jested,
Until one, with a whip, made him bellow.

A sun-bather staying at Weston,
Sat out on the beach, with his vest on,
His plans were frustrated
Being ordered, 'tis stated,
To get up and put all the rest on!

There was a young fellow of Yatton,
Who would go to church with his hat on;
'It's safer,' he said,
On the top of my head,
On a seat it's sure to be sat on!'

NORTON FITZWARREN CRASHES

A newspaper account of a railway accident on the Great Western Railway on the night of 11 November 1890 opened with the words: 'About 1.30 on Tuesday morning one of the most frightful railway accidents that has ever happened in the West of England occurred at Norton Fitzwarren Junction.' It occurred at a point about 2 miles beyond Taunton, where the branch lines to Minehead and Barnstaple forked away from the main line to Exeter. Unhappily, history was to repeat itself almost exactly fifty years later, when the 9.50 p.m. passenger train from Paddington was derailed at the same spot at 3.48 a.m. on 5 November 1940, resulting in twenty-seven people being killed and seventy-five injured. More deaths occurred in a sleeping car fire in the third disaster in the area in 1978.

The full newspaper account of the 1890 accident records:

> From statements made by railway officials it appears that the signalman in charge of the Norton box, whose name is George Rice, is an old servant of the Great Western Company, and has occupied the same position for 30 years. He went on duty Monday night about nine o'clock. Later on the first half of a special train from Plymouth, carrying a portion of the mail and passengers just landed from the Cape steamer, passed through, en route for London. Shortly after one a.m. the ordinary slow down goods train was shunted on to the up line to allow an express goods train to pass on its way to Plymouth.
>
> Rice, however, appears to have forgotten that the slow goods train was standing on the up line, for a few minutes later, when he received a message asking if the line was clear to allow the second half of the special Cape mail train to get through, he signalled that it was all clear. The Cape mail approached at 60 miles per hour, and seeing the signals clear, dashed through the station into the goods train standing just beyond. The driver and stoker of the goods train, named Charles Noble and Alfred Dowding respectively, saw with horror the express approaching. They blew their whistle and then leapt for their lives. Dowding had time to run several yards and get beneath a truck on a siding before the crash occurred.

> The scenes which followed are described by eyewitnesses as simply awful. The engines were completely locked, and the carriages were piled up to the height of nearly 30 feet. The mail consisted of a tank engine, two coaches and a guard's van. The first of the two coaches was smashed up like matchwood, and to add to the horror of the scene, the front carriage caught fire from the engine. The burning carriage, the two monster engines lying half athwart the line, the great piles of wreckage, the shrieks of the wounded and dying, made up in the pitch dark night, and the torrents of rain which were falling, a scene of horror which has seldom been equalled. Men in the front carriage, jambed [*sic*] under piles of wreckage, were uttering awful shrieks, and offering all the wealth of which they were possessed to the men who would rescue them.
>
> The work of rescue was quickly proceeded with. Mr Kemp, the stationmaster at Norton Fitzwarren, was aroused and sent off messages at once to arouse his staff. Telegrams were forwarded to Taunton, Exeter, Bristol and other places. Within four minutes of the receipt of the telegraph at Taunton a pilot engine with all available men on duty at Taunton Station was on its way to the scene of the accident. Within a few minutes of the occurrence many of the people who were alive were got out from the second carriage, but it was hours before some of those in the front carriage were rescued. The wreckage had to be torn to pieces bit by bit to get them out.
>
> The fire was soon extinguished, but the burns on some of the bodies show that several passengers met their death by the flames. One survivor states that in his compartment there were five other men, and he was the only one who escaped alive. By some miraculous chance he received scarcely any injury, while the others were all crushed to death. A lady and gentleman were in the last compartment of the first carriage, but though one side of the compartment was torn clean out, they all escaped unhurt. The total number of passengers was 47.
>
> The injury sustained by the front part of the goods train was rather serious. The engine was ruined. The truck next to the engine was, with the tender, forced across the down line, the truck being driven in the hedge. Just behind these was a truckload of corn, two wheels of which were driven about a foot into the ground, and the engine was partly on top of this truck. One truck was driven up on top of some other trucks in the siding.

Ten people died in this accident which, like the one fifty years later, was caused by human error. It may be significant that both occurred in the early hours of a Monday morning when signalmen and others would begin the first of their week of night turns. Add the darkness and heavy rain to the normal difficulties of their job and it is easier to understand how such errors might occur, especially with the additional blackout factor during wartime.

The third railway disaster in the Norton Fitzwarren area occurred in the early hours of 6 July 1987 and resulted in twelve fatalities. The deaths occurred as a result of a fire in a sleeping car, caused by a heater setting light to stored bed linen. This gave off carbon monoxide, which entered the air conditioning system and penetrated the compartments where the luckless passengers were asleep. Fire then broke out in the leading sleeper and rescuers had to overcome doors that had been locked for security reasons to help a fortunate few to safety.

O

OIL SHALE BUBBLE

In an article which appeared in 1924 Dr W. Forbes-Leslie optimistically wrote, 'It is a veritable new discovery – a class of oil shale hitherto unknown to exist in England, and of a thickness so great, and having an oil content so rich, as to astonish scientific investigators.' He was referring to the extensive shale deposits along the shore of the Bristol Channel between Watchet and Stolford, and quoted estimates made by consulting engineer Larrett C. Parkin that the deposits were capable of yielding an amazing 9,000 million tons of oil shale and 3,000 million tons of limestone. These remarkable forecasts followed limited test drilling near Kilve in 1920 and, had they proved reliable, would have transformed this quiet area of West Somerset into a huge industrial complex. As Forbes-Leslie dramatically put it, 'The hills can be blasted down, great faces opened hundreds of feet high, and the rich oil fuel picked up by steam shovels and loaded onto railway trucks for 3*s* a ton.'

In his article Forbes-Leslie went on to further extol the massive potential of the West Somerset shale beds, and calculated that the fuel they produced would be much cheaper than coal and be worth 'an aggregate value of about £3 billion.' And, as if that was not enough, the limestone in the adjoining beds could be fired by this cheap fuel and mixed with the burnt shale residue to produce a 'stronger and more durable' cement at about half the cost of the normal Portland variety. All this, said the eminent gentleman jingoistically, would be good for England and 'absorb a vast proportion of her unemployment, and automatically divert into the pockets of her workmen some of the millions which today are being lavished on foreigners, with disastrous results for ourselves, both socially and industrially.'

After a period of lease negotiations in 1922, the scheme received wide publicity in local and technical circles the following year, when the idea of a railway link to Bridgwater was also floated. By the end of that year the small experimental retort erected near Kilve was being dismantled in order to make room for a larger one, and the wave of optimism and ambition surrounding the project escalated even further with talk of building dozens of retorts to feed two large refineries, and even the establishment of a new dock at Combwich. A company called Shalime Ltd was launched to exploit the potential of the shale, and approaches made to both the Great Western Railway and the Government body responsible for considering financial loans for projects which would help to alleviate unemployment.

The Kilve oil shale retort minus its original side bands and linked condensers. The storage shed has also gone, leaving just a forlorn shell to mark what might have become a vast industrial complex.

By mid-1924 the Kilve retort was working. Excavated shale was crushed and fed in at the top of the 35ft high brick building to be then heated in an iron cylinder. The resultant gas was converted to a crude oil in condensers for subsequent refining as required. Apparently several hundred barrels of oil were produced, the first tangible results of some four years of development. Was this the realisation of Forbes-Leslie's prophecy that West Somerset's rich oil shale would place England 'at once in the front rank of cheap-fuel producing countries'?

By the end of that year, however, the great expectations of Forbes-Leslie and the Shalime company had all but evaporated. They had found that the shale was contaminated by sulphur and slag, that the burned residue could not be used for cement making and that the beds plunged too deeply for easy mining. A few optimists continued to discuss the possibilities of the coastal shale for a year or two, but the grand dream was over and the area remains untouched, with only the shell of the old brick retort house to mark the high hopes of the 1920s.

P

PACKETS, PADDLERS AND PIERS

Sea trips for pleasure were rare before the nineteenth century, but by its close were a thriving activity, especially in estuaries like the Bristol Channel. A catalyst for this change was the formation of the Bristol Steam Packet Company in 1822. It heralded the commencement of regular passenger-carrying services between Bristol, South Wales and Ireland. These expanded over the following years, serving the increasing need for business travel and gradually taking over the role of the sailing vessels which had traditionally supplied produce to the Bristol markets.

The first steam vessel operation in Somerset was along the River Avon between Bristol and Bath, but a new era dawned when the Greenock-built steam *Britannia* arrived in the Bristol Channel in May 1817. She was a sizeable vessel of 112 tons, fitted with both paddles and sails and commanded by a naval reserve officer, as was then the custom. Bristolians had the chance to join one of the excursions she made from the port. Before long, other steamers began to appear and soon sought to increase their earnings by fitting a few pleasure trips into spare hours in their regular packet boat services.

These were the pioneering years for steam propulsion, and the early vessels were liable to machinery failure and boiler explosions; partly because their design was rudimentary, and partly due to the inexperience of their engineers and stokers. It was the period when many a coastal observer believed the smoke from the funnels of these newcomers meant that they were on fire.

Paddle tugs soon joined in the move to offer pleasure trips. Their basic role was that of towing sailing vessels into and out of ports like Bristol and Bridgwater where the tidal range was so critical. Large, powerful and built on generous lines, these paddle tugs could be adapted for their spare time trip work by fitting extra decking and by erecting temporary awnings. Weston-super-Mare got its first steamer outing opportunity this way when the 85ton tug *Sampson* started offering short pleasure trips from Knightstone Harbour in the summer of 1843.

Among the dramatic changes in the nineteenth century was the growth of the seaside holiday habit, prompted by improving employment conditions, the spread of the railway system and many other factors.

These changes made the construction and operation of purpose-built pleasure vessels a viable proposition. The new generation of paddle steamers could carry more people with better accommodation and greater reliability. They were to be a feature of the Somerset coastal scene right up until after the Second World War. The boom in pleasure trips produced an immense variety of vessels, intense rivalry between operators and not a few dramatic incidents.

This former public house sign at Burnham-on-Sea captures an era when the Somerset & Dorset Railway operated its own steamers and a line extended beyond the station onto the steamer pier to enable wagons to be loaded or unloaded there. For a brief early period travellers could use the route to travel from Cardiff to Paris via Poole and Cherbourg.

To be able to land and board passengers despite tidal restraint meant building piers out into deeper waters. Within four years of the arrival of the railway, increasing visitor numbers prompted a Weston-super-Mare project to build a pier out to Birnbeck Island. By 1846, an enabling Act had been obtained, with work then starting on an elegant suspension design by James Dredge in 1847. Sadly, by the end of that year a terrible storm had destroyed the works and, along with them, the hopes of both engineer and promoters.

A happier outcome was achieved twenty years later with the opening of a pier designed by Eugenius Birch, the engineer for the pier at Brighton, on 5 June 1867. Fifteen iron supporting piers carried the cantilever spans of a 1,040ft walkway from shore to Birnbeck Island, with a 250ft wooden landing stage extension beyond for the steamer passengers. Later on, the latter was replaced with new metal structures which enabled vessels to berth at both low and high tides. Weston's new attraction had cost £67,775, but was soon bringing large numbers of extra visitors to the resort.

Recent years have seen this pioneer pier, unique in incorporating an island, deteriorating and with an uncertain future, but in its heyday as many as 15,000 people a day might land there from the paddle steamers queuing up to unload. There was a lot of competition between the captains of these vessels, with the odd minor collision serving to enliven the day for the spectators. Some of the steamer passengers would stay on in Weston, but most would return on foot or by seafront tram after a day enjoying the beaches and other seaside attractions of

Weston-super-Mare's first pier out to Birnbeck Island, with a steamer at one of its two extensions and with a launch ramp leading down from the lifeboat building.

the town. Each summer evening there would be some frantic scrambling to avoid missing the boats, made all the more frenetic by the steamers using their sirens to urge would-be passengers to greater haste.

There was so much to do on Birnbeck Pier in its best years. The 1884 pavilion and reading rooms were soon outmoded by swings, mechanical models and marvels, a shooting gallery and a merry-go-round, with even more sophisticated entertainments being installed later. These included a switchback, cakewalk, slides and helter-skelter plus more dramatic rides like the flying chariots and the water chute. Visitors could also enjoy the luncheon and tea rooms, listen to the band or dance in the theatre-cum-ballroom.

Birnbeck Pier survived fire in 1897 and gale damage in 1903, but the opening of the Grand Pier in Weston then robbed it of the many visitors who wanted the latter's nearby beach and shops. During the Second World War, as *HMS Birnbeck*, the pier hosted the so-called 'Wheezers and Dodgers', who developed specialised weapons in great secrecy there. The pier remained fairly popular with Welsh steamer visitors until the end of the P & A Campbell services in 1979. After that it did struggle on for a while longer, but then was closed to all but the crews of the lifeboat station, first established there in 1882.

Somerset's second pier was built at Clevedon. The resort had been growing in population and visitor numbers since the arrival of the branch railway from Yatton in 1847, and leading citizens soon began to feel that a pier was needed to fulfil their aspirations for the town. The result was a Parliamentary Bill which was considered and approved in the 1863-64 session. The resultant

842ft pier was finally opened on Easter Monday in 1869 with every conceivable organisation taking part, supposedly 130 speeches, and local children enjoying the gift of a threepenny piece and a bun. The delicate structure was approached through a splendid toll house and an equally unique structure was added at the steamer end in 1894.

Clevedon pier proved popular in its early years, but maintenance costs began to eat into the profits by the 1890s when it was gifted to the town of Clevedon through the generosity of Sir Edmund Elton. As tastes changed it ceased to be viable in the 1950s and then had to be closed when a span collapsed during routine testing in October 1970. After ten years of neglect, authority was sought for abandonment, but at a public inquiry the inspector supported the proposals of the Clevedon Pier Preservation Trust to begin a period of heroic effort which brought about the reopening of the pier in May 1989. In the following years it became a regular calling place for the surviving Channel pleasure cruise activity.

Back in Weston-super-Mare there was talk of a second pier nearer the town and railway as early as 1880, but it took another twenty-three years before work actually started. In the meantime, the pier at Minehead was opened in 1901. It was a fairly plain structure with a steamer extension, which handled regular sailings to and from South Wales and on the Bristol to Lundy and Ilfracombe routes. The pier was highly popular in the years between the wars, but was then demolished in 1940 to avoid interference with defences on the

Beyond Knightstone Island and the sailing vessels using the harbour is Weston's Grand Pier, pictured before removal of the long extension which steamer operators found did not solve the berthing problems caused by exposure and the difficult tidal conditions.

West Somerset coast. Apparently it obstructed the field of fire of a defensive gun battery, but there are suggestions that the ancient weapon involved was not capable of firing anyway! The steamship company owners of Minehead pier had plans to rebuild it post-war, but nothing came of these.

In Weston-super-Mare the scheme for a new pier finally came to life. When it did, things moved quickly, with the 1,080ft main structure and 2,000-seat end pavilion opening on 11 June 1904.

A short-lived 1,500ft extension was added in 1907, but the combination of exposed position, strong currents and big tidal range led to the steamer companies deciding that they could not berth there and continuing to use Birnbeck. For many years the theatre was the big attraction on the Grand Pier, with performances as varied as music hall and grand opera, ballet and boxing, and with such stars as Anna Pavlova, Vesta Tilley and Ralph Richardson. Despite the steamer companies withdrawing their services from 1908 because the tides and currents in Weston Bay made mooring dangerous, the pier continued to be popular. After a terrible fire in 1930 the pavilion was rebuilt as a funfair and continued to attract thousands of visitors every year until another fire in 2008 destroyed the end pavilion and precipitated another rebuilding. This reopened two years later, thanks to a design which seemed to meet with universal approval.

PIGEON PIE

The Romans used pigeons as a valuable food source and the Norman conquerors brought the practice of harvesting both pigeons and rabbits on a significant scale to Britain, the former farmed in pigeon lofts or dovecotes and the latter in dedicated warrens. Pigeon lofts tend to be referred to as dovecotes, although doves are actually smaller members of the same bird family.

Until the beginning of the seventeenth century, the right to have a dovecote was confined to the aristocracy, lords of the manor, religious houses and parish priests. Indeed, it was not unknown for pigeons to be housed in a church tower or steeple. Among the forty-two dovecotes listed by Dom Ethelbert Horne as surviving in Somerset was one over the chancel of the parish church at Compton Martin, and others at Witham Friary and Hinton Charterhouse abbey ruins.

Until root crops became available to provide winter feed for cattle, pigeons were a prime source of meat. Unsurprisingly, the monopoly enjoyed by the manor and the clergy was increasingly resented and flouted, and eventually ended in 1619. However, as the population expanded and corn crops started to have a critical effect on the nation's well-being, pigeons could no longer be allowed to feed freely over cultivated land. By the time of the long years of war with France from 1793, corn harvests had become critical; pigeons were actively discouraged and dovecotes fell steadily into disuse. Those that have survived are generally the more substantial ones which were part of a manor farm.

The dovecotes used by the Normans were mostly solidly built and circular with a domed roof. Later designs began to vary considerably and the practice of having a separate building was often modified to include provision for pigeon keeping as part of a barn or other building. The recorded Somerset dovecotes varied in size from forty nests in the hilltop building at Bruton to 1,236 nests at Cathanger Manor House Farm at Fivehead. The normal capacity seems to have been between 450 and 750 nests, although there are some examples of much higher figures.

Standard dovecote features included a small entrance door and a roof aperture which could be opened and closed to permit the birds to enter or leave. Ventilation was important and normally provided by roof louvres, while a small window would let in enough light to enable the man in charge to see what he was doing. Around the inside of the dovecote there would be holes in the stone or brickwork shaped to accommodate a pigeon comfortably, usually provided with a ledge or small perch for alighting. From a central post an arm or arms, sometimes supporting a platform, radiated out to the wall, with a ladder at the end to facilitate access to any of the nests by revolving the whole structure. When needed for the table, the birds would be disturbed and then

The interior of the dovecote at Dunster showing the access platform and ladder and the roosting inlets.

trapped in a short-handled net. To take the youngest birds for the delicacy of a squab pie, the ladder would have to be used.

Pigeon pie was a tasty dish and in later years could be had at any decent inn, not just on the manor farm table. However, the concept of keeping birds which fed from other peoples' corn and seed did not sit well with those who had to suffer the consequent replanting and poor harvests. The only remedy they had was bird scaring, which came to be the prerogative of young lads armed with a homemade rattle and keening a refrain which was meant to scare, and not to entertain. No doubt they also managed to trap a few birds for their own pigeon pie!

PIRATES OFFSHORE

In the years before the Norman Conquest, the periodic raiding incursions of Nordic seafarers subjected the coastal settlements of Somerset to their insatiable search for plunder. The more adventurous, travelling further up the Bristol Channel, would have rounded Middle Hope and eyed the green pastures around Woodspring Bay which they could easily explore and exploit by probing up the Yeo and Banwell rivers. By 1636 those early dramas would have meant little to the inhabitants of the tiny hamlet of Wick St Lawrence, but they were in for a rude shock.

As trade had increased and the number of vessels sailing the Channel waters had risen, so had the ranks of those intent on robbing them. Piracy was mentioned in the *Anglo-Saxon Chronicle*, and one petition to authority complained, 'There are five Turks in the Severn, where they weekly take … a great number of ships in

The mouth of the Banwell River and Woodspring Bay beyond look peaceful enough these days, but once attracted marauders and smugglers.

the Channel.' Royal advice in 1266 was simply that legitimate shipping should travel in convoy, but Henry V did, at least, establish officials with power to punish offences at sea. This did not have much of an effect, and by the fifteenth century raiders had even established shore bases, including Milford Haven, Tenby, Penarth and Cardiff. Parliament was told about 'Welshmen and ill-disposed persons who assembled in manner of war and stopped trows, boats, floats or drags … (They would) hew in pieces these craft and beat the sailors with intent to force them to hire boats from the said Welshmen for great sums of money.'

Despite the appointment of Piracy Commissioners, things got worse. The commissioners could issue licences to hunt pirates for a share in any goods captured, but the pickings for freebooters were just too tempting. Raiders from Algeria who had formerly waited for their prey off Land's End became more adventurous. Soon a motley array of Barbary, Ottoman, Moorish, Turkish and other corsairs were using shallow draught vessels with sweeps and square sails to probe every corner of the Bristol Channel where defenceless victims were to be found. During the many wars French, Dunkirk and Biscay pirates operated as privateers under licence from their governments and even reached as far up-Channel as the Holms. All the intruders managed to vanish when British warships appeared, but quickly reappeared as soon as these were reassigned.

An especially unsavoury feature of the activities of the Barbary Coast galleys was the brutal coastal raids they made in search of valuables, supplies and, sometimes, slaves. Typical of these incidents was one involving the tiny hamlet of Wick St Lawrence in 1636. The peace of its rural existence was shattered one day by the sudden arrival of swarthy intruders who had sailed up the little River Yeo, intent on taking prisoners to augment their rowing complement or who could be sold after they had returned home. On some occasions those captured could be bought back with payments on the spot, but the many collections and legacies directed to raising money 'for the ransom of Christian slaves from the Moors' reveal that others were not so fortunate. The maiming of victims who would not convert to Islam was not unknown.

With so many European wars in the eighteenth century, the Bristol Channel rarely enjoyed a long, settled spell. Many ships were taken, especially by French privateers, but at least one of the latter, the *Grand Joseph*, failed to evade capture and was taken into Minehead. Not that these activities were one-sided, for Minehead also had three privateers at sea in the Spanish War of Succession, one a 200-ton, 16-gun galley.

By the time the Sea Fencibles force was created in 1798 to protect the coast from any French invasion, the navy was strong enough to bottle up potential privateers in their home ports and piracy was largely at an end. Smuggling became the new thing, with Penarth and Flat Holm pivotal to duty-evading activities. Full law and order still lay some way ahead for navigators in the Bristol Channel.

POIGNANT GRAVES

In a corner of the churchyard of St Peter's parish church at Portishead, beside a busy footpath, but rarely noticed, is a forgotten group of three graves. Beneath their worn stones and the creeping vegetation lie the remains of thirteen young boys whose ages ranged from sixteen to as young as eleven. One of the gravestones, still legible, records the last resting place of two thirteen-year-olds: Henry Martin, who died in May 1871, and Henry James Roach, whose life ended six months later. Eight boys who died between 1873 and 1877 are recorded on another stone, with four more on a slab alongside.

These boys came from the training ship *Formidable*, which was moored off Portishead and used to train 'street arabs' from Bristol for a more useful life as seamen. The vessel itself was a redundant 84-gun, two-decker naval ship-of-line, built in 1825. She could accommodate 300 pupils. Their seagoing tuition was given on board a two-masted, former fruit trade brig called *Polly*.

The scheme to retrain Bristol's abandoned and destitute lads originated in 1869, thanks to the efforts of Henry Fedden, chairman of the city's Board of Magistrates at the time, who was greatly concerned about the number of boys coming before the courts. They were a sorry mixture of orphans, the poor, the undernourished and a generally neglected class that Fedden aimed to see converted to useful lives.

The boys sent from the courts to *Formidable* received clothing, meals, accommodation and schooling in seamanship and general subjects. They worked hard, starting at 5.30 a.m. in summer and 6.30 a.m. in winter, and were subject to severe discipline, but their health was always a major consideration and steadily benefited from their improved circumstances. The floating school fitted thousands for a new and useful life, but it operated in a tough environment and the sea, the high rigging and the diseases of the times all claimed their victims, like the thirteen who lie in the Portishead graveyard.

The faded legends on these gravestones at Portishead record the sad deaths of thirteen young boys aged from eleven to sixteen.

Old age eventually led to the abandonment of the ex-warship in favour of a substantial building ashore in 1903. This, in turn, eventually closed in the early 1980s and was converted to residential apartments.

POULTER AKA BAXTER

John Poulter, who also used the name Baxter, was born in Newmarket in 1715 and went to work for the Duke of Somerset as a stable boy when he was thirteen. His early career amid the horses and hounds of the gentry took him to France and gave him a taste for travel, with later voyages to Africa and America. Perhaps envious of the riches he had seen in the hands of others, he later turned to a life of villainy based in a small inn building near Box in Wiltshire. There he added a new window, through which he could watch for potential victims using the Corston road.

At least two of Poulter's crimes were carried out over the county boundary in Somerset. Unfortunately for him one of these was to lead to his arrest, trial and execution, a process that was to reveal Poulter as a man of considerable, if dubious, character.

On Wednesday 21 March 1753 an eminent physician, one Doctor Hancock of Salisbury, was travelling on a lonely stretch of road at Claverton Down, near Bath. With him in the carriage was his young granddaughter, who was greatly distressed when Poulter and his gang suddenly held them up at pistol point. It is recorded that Poulter was very gentle with the distraught young girl, a feature which led Doctor Hancock to speak up for him later on. Even so, the gang still relieved the doctor of anything worth having about his person and in his luggage, including a gold watch and some silver plate.

It became clear later that Poulter's network of villainy was quite extensive, for some of Dr Hancock's possessions were recovered from Bath silversmith John Ford and others from John Roberts, who kept the Pack Horse Inn there. Immediately after the robbery, the Poulter gang had returned to their main base at the Wiltshire inn to sort over the loot and replenish their supplies. Poulter himself then headed off towards Exeter to look for his next victim.

This information (and more) came out when Poulter, betrayed by one of his gang for a newspaper reward, was arrested at Exeter on the Tuesday after the Claverton Down incident. With indecent haste he named his suppliers and fences and offered up the details of every member of his gang. This included two men recently returned from transportation and two women. All this was recorded in affidavits which Poulter signed on the day immediately following his capture. He seems to have believed firmly that the route out of his troubles was that of disclosures, for a small book of these was written while he was in prison at Taunton, and several other pamphlets were penned before his eventual execution.

This extraordinary highwayman was tried at the Assizes at Wells and duly convicted there on 28 August 1753. He was housed in Ilchester Gaol to await his execution, which was fixed for 1 November. But the incredible Poulter was by no means ready to give up. Somehow he persuaded the civic officials at Taunton to submit a strong petition for his release and followed it up with one of his own. The latter declared that he had revealed the names of thirty-five other thieves, sixteen of whom had already been arrested. The pleas seemed to work, for they earned a reprieve on two occasions.

Four months after his conviction Poulter was still being held in the prison at Ilchester. He appears to have enjoyed some freedom of movement there, probably encouraged by his self-belief and the expectation that his revelations would lead to some easement of his condemned status. A woman prisoner in the back yard had cause to be thankful for this when she upset a candle and set some straw alight, for Poulter was able to rescue her and raise the alarm before the fire became serious.

Unfortunately for the highwayman, his time was running out. A new execution date was fixed for 18 February and Poulter was then placed in irons and watched during the night to make sure that he was secure. The leg irons caused bad sores on the prisoner's ankles so, to afford him some relief for one leg at a time, he was chained to a fellow inmate, a debtor named Newman.

By the day before that fixed for his execution Poulter was desperate. He offered to make further disclosures, an offer that seems to have encouraged the guards to relax the constant surveillance, for at 10 p.m. the chained pair managed to prize a bar out of the cell window, hobble together over the roof and lower themselves into a garden beyond the prison wall. Still linked together by 28lbs of iron chain, they covered some 10 miles before finding the tools to get the shackles off.

The escape caused immediate panic when discovered. The age-old 'Hue and Cry' was instigated, messengers were sent out to strategic points like the ferry passage to Wales and the local newspapers were asked to publish details of the wanted men. Poulter was discovered near Wells and brought back to Ilchester where an order for his execution was received at 2 p.m. on the afternoon of Sunday 24 February. The event was quickly arranged for the following morning.

Early on the Monday, Poulter received the Sacrament from the Vicar of Martock and was placed, with his coffin, on the cart that was to take him along the Yeovil Road to Gallows Acre Field. Arriving there, showman to the last, he made a short speech welcoming death, acknowledged an old crony in the watching crowd and assured everyone of the truth of the pamphlets he had written. Next, this extraordinary man climbed on top of his coffin, asked the executioner to shorten the rope around his neck and, when this had been done, leapt into space rather than wait for the cart to be drawn out from under him.

And so ended the life of highwayman Poulter. His legacy to Edward Clothier and John Cox, who ran Ilchester Gaol from 1732 to 1756, was the necessity of writing two reports to explain his escape and defend themselves against charges

(From a Thomas Bewick woodcut)

that they had accepted bribes of twenty guineas to facilitate it. They were obliged to detail all they had done to keep Poulter secure, but also pleaded that improvements were badly needed to their 'weak bad prison'. They also revealed that the debtors housed there more or less did as they liked and had connived in the bribery allegations just to cause trouble. The gaolers had to get the two clergymen who had attended Poulter to certify that he had withdrawn the bribery story in his last confession.

Doubtless Clothier and Cox were glad to reach the end of the Poulter saga, although the book he wrote in Taunton Gaol in May must have continued to haunt them, for it ran to at least ten editions. Poulter had invited Beau Nash to endorse these writings, but that gentleman declined the honour. Despite his years of crime, John Poulter seems to deserve a little admiration for his imagination and persistence, but there is also evidence that while working for Archdeacon of Wells, Dr George Shakerley, he shot that poor gentleman while he was taking an afternoon nap, robbed him of his ready cash and then placed a pistol in the unfortunate clergyman's hand to suggest suicide.

Q

QUAINT TRAINS

Weston-super-Mare was linked to the infant British railway system quite early on, but not quite in the way it would have wanted. The town did get a railway line and station, but only a rather second-rate affair. This was because creating a new railway was an expensive business involving survey, legal, Parliamentary and land purchase costs in addition to the actual building and equipment expenses. Branch lines were certainly needed to feed in additional revenue-earning traffic, but finding the additional capital for them was another matter.

When the Bristol & Exeter Railway opened its main line as far as Bridgwater in 1841, it was already planning to add branch lines as finance permitted. The first addition, also in 1841, was to the growing town of Weston-super-Mare, but this had to be done on the cheap. With the main line taking a direct and easy course inland and just behind the town, the solution was a short branch line.

The new railway to Weston-super-Mare was just a single track from a modest junction on the main line and terminating in an equally modest station near the town centre. The disappointing feature for the Town Commissioners was not only that there would be no through trains, but that the line was equipped with very basic coaches and those were to be pulled by horses! The distance involved was only 1½ miles, but speed rarely exceeded 2mph and many potential passengers found they could walk the distance more quickly.

Weston's quaint horse-drawn trains worked the line for ten years. The motive power was three horses in tandem, animals rarely in their prime and ridden by young boys of limited experience and sometimes less sense. They hauled three small coaches with hard wooden seats and minimal cover to provide a journey tolerable in summer, but highly uncomfortable in bad weather.

Not surprisingly, accidents often occurred on this second-rate railway. An account of a mishap in 1847 states, 'one of the horses, suffering from a diseased heart, fell upon the rails and the carriages passed over it, causing immediate death. The train was thrown off the line and the passengers finished the journey on foot.' A bad year was to follow in 1849. On 9 January, the third in the line of horses of an evening train to the town fell and had a foot cut off by the following coaches.

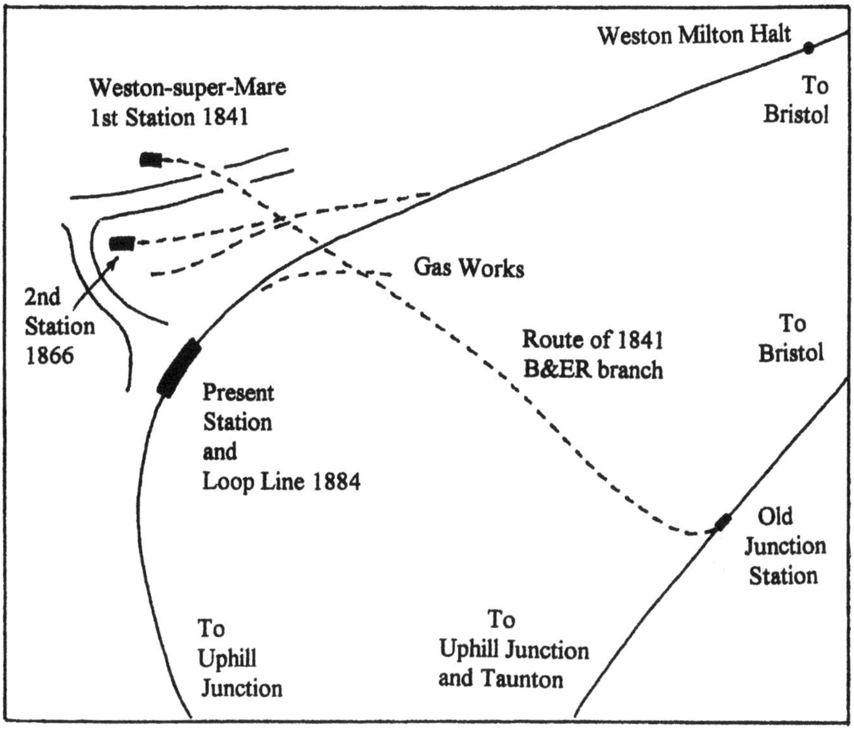

The various railway lines at Weston-super-Mare.

Later, a lead horse was decapitated in a derailment in which the rider also failed to escape, a report recording, 'one of the boy's legs was run up by a wheel, whilst the other leg was pinned under the dead animal's body.' In yet another mishap, two more horses were badly injured.

By now the railway users had had enough. Pressure on the company had already led to the provision of a morning through express and an evening counterpart, both being hauled by locomotives, and in 1851 all the services began to be worked this way. Subsequently, the access line to Weston became double track, a new approach line and terminus was built in 1866 and a through station on a loop line in 1884.

Horse power did not entirely forsake the Weston railway scene in 1851 however; an old coach drawn by a horse hired from a local farmer continued to be used to take the evening mails to the junction station for some years.

QUIRKE'S CURSE

The Quirke family of Minehead were prominent seafarers, taking the barrels of herrings caught by local fishermen to distant markets. This was a major activity in the sixteenth and seventeenth centuries, with hundreds of barrels of fish being shipped out; not only the regular supplies to Bristol, but some dispatched to destinations as far afield as the Mediterranean. On one of these occasions around 1630 Robert Quirke, along with his brother, was caught in a terrible storm as they sailed back to their home port. Their small vessel was so tossed about that they feared for its survival and their lives.

The row of Quirke's almshouses occupies a convenient position near the centre of Minehead.

On their knees, the two brothers prayed for deliverance and Robert vowed to sell their vessel and its cargo, and devote the proceeds to the poor of his hometown if they were spared. Miraculously, the storm abated and the battered vessel was able to limp home.

True to his promise, Robert Quirke sold the cargo, disposed of the vessel and used the proceeds, together with some of the ship's timbers, to build a row of eleven small almshouses for the poor of his hometown. There was a small turret at one end incorporating a bell, said to be from the ship which had survived the storm and provided the funds.

There was also a plaque which read:

Robert Qvirke sonne of James Qvirke
Built this house ano : 1630 : and
Doth give it to the vse of the poore
Of this parish for ever and for better
Maintenance doe give my two inner
Sellers at the inner end of the key
And cursed be that man that shall
Convert it to any other use than
The vse of the poore 1630

The 'sellers' were warehouses on the quay at Minehead, subsequently converted into a chapel and sailors' shelter. The eleven almshouses themselves were subsequently converted into eight more modernised homes, but they still serve their founders' intention, and Quirke's curse has not been invoked.

R

RETAIL THERAPY

It took many centuries for retailing, as we now know it, to emerge from its origins with individual craftsmen selling their products from ground floor or basement 'work shops'. The period in between was the province of fairs and markets and of the itinerant pedlars, hawkers, chapmen and 'Scotsmen' who frequented them and toured the countryside between events. These travelling salesmen were a major feature by the nineteenth century. Many obtained their supplies, often clothing, from town or port warehouses and then sold them to cottagers throughout Somerset, sometimes accepting payment in instalments. Collecting the instalments fortnightly led to these men becoming known as 'Johnny Fornightlies', and some did so well that they could travel with their own pony and trap. Other traders sold specialist items such as watches at the fairs and markets, often using a form of mock auction and a great deal of patter.

Conventional shops began to appear as transport and trade improved, Bath being quick to provide retail outlets to cater for the increasing number of visitors. Libraries and bookshops were early examples, while Wedgewood and others set up showrooms to tempt the wealthy. Medical men were numerous in the city, resulting in the establishment of dispensaries to discharge their prescriptions and also to offer the growing number of patent remedies; some, like Daffy's Elixir, offering the promise of curing almost any ailment.

When he conducted his tea business from this house in South Petherton, Samuel McMillan had his name and activity nicely carved over the doorway.

Retailing was somewhat less sophisticated in rural Somerset, where shops were frequently set up in the front room of ordinary houses. A tea dealer in South Petherton displayed his name and trade on the door lintel, taking his supplies from the chapmen who served the importers and merchants, and offering it packeted to local callers or those of sufficient status to warrant a delivery.

John Tonkin used bricks and tiles from his own brickyard when he built this magnificent emporium in Wedmore around 1830.

A notable exception to village retail simplicity occurred in Wedmore, where John Tonkin, a Cornish businessman, funded an impressive new venture from the proceeds of a brickyard which he built there. Tonkin purchased a small shop near the church and demolished it to make way for a magnificent emporium: a fine Italianate building of three storeys. Inside were a grocery section to cater for everyday requirements, homeware and fashion departments to encourage less essential spending, and even a bank. Clients came from miles around to view the latest fashions bought in by Mrs Tonkin and to take tea in the now-lost tower as a break from a session in the fitting rooms.

The twentieth century marked the advent of department stores and the reinvention of retail shopping they encouraged. Even so, there are still shops around displaying a rare period frontage, with examples in Ilminster and Bridgwater. One well-known store in Weston-super-Mare still has, in working order but used only for stock control, the pneumatic tubes which used to link sales floor staff with the hidden cashier.

S

SMALL SPAS

The medicinal spas of Bath and Bristol grew in patronage throughout the eighteenth century and reached the height of their popularity in the first part of the nineteenth. Large numbers sought the health treatments they offered and the social life that had become an integral part of the spa 'season'. Less well-known is the fact that four smaller, but highly individual, spa establishments were set up in Somerset, although none competed with the fashionable entertainments and other trappings that were such an important feature of a visit to one of their more illustrious counterparts.

Although widely used as a treatment for gout, drinking the waters at Bath tended to have costive consequences and, as early as 1676, water from Alford Well, near Castle Cary, was being bottled and distributed specifically to counteract this. Later the well acquired a bad reputation and fell into disuse. Another spring with an early medicinal reputation was one near Queen Camel, which had rudimentary facilities for bathing around 1750. Quite a few other wells and springs enjoyed local reputations for healing conditions as varied as gastric disorders, skin ailments and eye problems.

The waters of the Chalice Well at Glastonbury, which had supplied the great abbey there during its lifetime, were to receive considerable notoriety in 1751 as a result of the dramatic cure of yeoman Matthew Chancellor's asthma in the previous year. Soon hundreds of people were coming for treatment and the water was being bottled and sold locally and in London. Anne Galloway, familiar with the spas at both Bath and Cheltenham, soon saw an opportunity to exploit the new-found popularity of the Glastonbury water.

Her plans featured in various newspaper advertisements at this time, inviting subscribers for the first season and promising a 'commodious pump-house and baths' and the availability of lodgings nearby. The pump house was certainly built and indeed still stands, but the venture only lasted a few years, seemingly due to its failure to replicate the impressive list of cures which the advertisements had claimed for the Glastonbury waters.

The long years of war with France, when English people were unable to visit the European spas, led to a great upsurge in the popularity of home establishments.

The ornate entrance to the former pump room at Glastonbury which was fed from the other side of the road with the same water source that had formerly supplied the abbey.

Noting this, many a landowner began to wonder whether the local healing reputation of a spring on his land could be exploited to cater for the spa habit.

The spa at Horwood Well House, just outside Wincanton, had an even more direct link with affairs in Europe, as French prisoners of war were among its clientele for several years. These were wealthy officers and colonials captured far from their homeland, placed on parole and accommodated in Wincanton when it became a parole town in 1806. Many still had access to their money, and their need for entertainment would have been readily apparent to the prominent local people who acquired the Horwood property and set out to provide spa facilities for the prisoners. Horwood was about 1 mile from the town, the movement limit imposed on PoWs by their parole conditions.

There were two wells at Horwood, both with a reputation for healing. A charming two-storey house was built over one of them, with a pleasant public room for taking the waters on the ground floor, a small bathing facility nearby and six bedrooms above. A short distance away, a second building had a chapel, coach house and stables on the lower floor with a dormitory and treatment rooms overhead. A small banking house was also set up in the grounds

Unhappily, the good times at Horwood failed to last. Both the Horwood Well bank and the main Wincanton bank were in trouble by 1810, with matters getting worse when the French patrons of the spa were allowed to return home. By 1819 the venture had come to the end of its brief popularity, and Horwood Well House was up for sale.

The decorative entrance to Horwood Well House would once have welcomed wealthy French prisoners of war lodged in Wincanton on parole during the Napoleonic conflict.

While the Horwood spa was failing, another venture was starting up, this time based on an analysis of water from a well dug in 1815 at Capland near Taunton. The analysis showed the water to have similar properties to those of the spa at Cheltenham. It was soon being bottled and sold locally, with callers being offered it by the glass for a penny.

As the fame of Capland Spa spread, more and more visitors arrived. To cater for those requiring an extended course of treatment, its owner, Thomas Walker, decided to add an extension to the main building. He also installed three furnaces in the well room to evaporate the well water and retail it as salts in packeted form.

The words 'Capland Spa', carved above the entrance, are a reminder of a former role of this pleasant house.

As small spas go, Capland had quite a long existence, only ceasing its activities in 1856 when its owner collapsed and died. By then the conventional spa industry as a whole was on the wane, although Somerset's largest spa facility, at Burnham-on-Sea, described in an earlier piece, was to continue in business for a few years longer.

The supposed healing properties of various other natural springs throughout Somerset acquired some small status and minor exploitation in the years when medicine was in its infancy, and cures more a matter of experiment than of treatment. Both legend and custom surrounded some of the wells, but their waters today have little standing, except in cases like the Chalice Well at Glastonbury.

STOCKS

For some 500 years the stocks were a familiar part of life in the towns and villages of this country. A period in the stocks was a commonplace means of restraining the over-exuberant and punishing the minor wrongdoer. Like lock-ups, a surprising number of stocks have survived in Somerset: at least eighteen are known, and there may be more. Not that this is evidence of excessive misbehaviour, for the records suggest that their use was never very frequent and eventually expired altogether.

When mason Tom Trout went to Trull church on a Sunday morning in December 1852 he was drunk and behaved badly. Hustled outside, he had to reflect on this in the stocks as he sat in the cold and snow until released at 2 p.m.

Stocks date back to Saxon times, but their general introduction followed a statute of 1351. This was passed as a direct result of the plague years of 1348 and 1349 which decimated the labour force and caused wages to rocket. To restrain the inflationary and destabilising consequences, the 1351 legislation laid down detention penalties of up to three days in the stocks for anyone demanding or paying higher wages. Every significant town, and later every village and manor, was required to provide stocks for this purpose.

Later centuries added vagabonds to the list of those eligible for confinement in the stocks, with a sentence of up to three days on bread and water rations, doubled in the event of reoffending. An Act of 1572 provided for the detention of 'rogues under 14', but the vicious confinement periods were getting less and a routine drunkenness conviction usually resulted in either a fine of 5*s* or six hours in the stocks. Ducking stools, pillories and whipping posts were the other main instruments of 'instant' punishment for minor offences, the stocks being used for the drunkards, profane and quarrelsome, whipping posts for rogues and petty thieves, the pillory for trade cheats and the ducking stool for scolding and other domestic complaints.

The stocks in Martock were originally located between the Pinnacle and the Market House, and in 1859 were ordered for intoxicated chimney sweep Joseph Gillard who served four hours for insulting two ladies and failing to pay

A young girl who messed about with the church organ spent a brief period in these stocks at West Monkton to teach her a lesson.

his 8*s* fine. It had been so long since their previous use that the lock could not be found and two constables had to stand guard to make sure the prisoner served his time! Lesson learned though, for Gillard later stated that 'he would rather sweep a dozen chimneys than go in the stocks again.' The Martock stocks today stand by the church wall, having survived a starring role in the testing of a fire extinguisher! The Glastonbury stocks were unusual in having wheels and could be positioned wherever required and those at West Monkton still have restraint shackles nearby. Other stocks were mostly locally made to a broadly standard design with four to six apertures between two hinged planks. Some, curiously, had an uneven number of holes.

At Wells in 1649 Anne Morgan's behaviour led to her being described as 'a widow of careless living'. Exactly what that entailed is not in the records; just her punishment of being 'imprisoned until Saturday's market, and then to be set in the stockes, and after that tyme to be washed in the Palace Moote, and then to be brought down to the prison, and there to remayne during the pleasure of the Mayor and Justice.'

With the establishment of a county police force with its police stations, cells and courts, stocks became redundant. Perhaps they were missed a little, for they had their uses; inhabitants of the Hundred of North Petherton once complained that in nine local parishes the stocks were 'in much decay for want of reparations', and secured a rate levy for their repair.

STUCKEY STORY

Prominent on the main road through Highbridge is an ornate red-brick building, faced with Ham Hill stone and built in 1877 to house a branch of Stuckey's Bank. It survives as a reminder of one of the most notable names in Somerset business and a quite remarkable story of enterprise. It all began when Samuel George Stuckey was born in Langport in 1740. By the time young Stuckey had reached his twenties, he was a successful general merchant with premises beside the River Parrett at Bow Bridge, and bringing goods up river by barge from Bridgwater to be unloaded at the Langport quay and distributed for many miles around.

Samuel George's dealings, especially in salt, brought rapid growth to the business, in which he was joined by solicitor's son Thomas Bagehot. Their combined talents, plus some good corn harvests to provide return barge loads to Bridgwater, accelerated the expansion of Stuckey & Bagehot, which was soon operating a sizeable fleet and dealing in a wide range of commodities. By now the Stuckey & Bagehot concern was frequently using written notes instead of cash, and setting up a bank was a predictable development.

Stuckey's Bank, Highbridge.

In 1806 Samuel George and his elder brother established the bank of S. & G. Stuckey with branches at Bristol and Bridgwater. By acquisition and amalgamation, Stuckey's Banking Co. came to have branches in most towns in Somerset until finally acquired by Parr's Bank in 1909. George's son Vincent and great-grandson, Vincent Stuckey Wood (alongside Ambrose Lethbridge and Thomas Watson Bagehot), steered this highly respected firm throughout the whole of the nineteenth century, ably managing its remarkable empire of banking, barging, seagoing shipping and the Somerset Trading Co.

SWIFTSURE

In 1840, just before the Bristol & Exeter Railway was opened to Bridgwater, the journey from there to London took thirteen and a half hours. The Swiftsure coach, described by one writer as 'the pride of the town' and 'well-horsed, well-equipped within and without and thoroughly well-driven', departed from outside the Clarence Hotel every Monday, Wednesday and Friday at 7.30 a.m. Travelling via Street, Glastonbury, Wells, Shepton Mallet, Frome, Warminster, Amesbury and Andover, it eventually reached the Bell and Crown Inn in Holborn at 9 p.m. There were frequent changes of horses, the Bridgwater driver handing over the reins at Andover and then waiting to bring the return horses back. These return journeys were made in the same timings on the following day.

A lady who died aged 100 in 1925 described a journey on this famous coach:

> In the days of my childhood a journey to London was a troublesome business. Those who could afford it went in post-chaises, others by coach. One had to rise very early, about four a.m. and I remember watching them trying to strike a light with a flint and tinder, lucifer matches being unknown. When a light was obtained a homemade tallow dip or rushlight would be lit, and after an early breakfast we would drive in a gig to Bridgwater, where we joined the famous express coach-and-four, the Swiftsure, which started from Bridgwater at 6.0 a.m. and reached London a distance of about 140 miles by ten or twelve that night. This was considered then a wonderfully rapid journey. The guard of the coach was always armed as one was quite likely to encounter highwaymen. Later in life I met a lady older than myself, who had once in her youth, when she was extremely beautiful, been compelled to dance a minuet with a highwayman in the moonlight, as the condition of retaining her jewels. She had also danced at the Waterloo Ball on which day one of my sisters was born.
>
> The Swiftsure was driven by a Mr Jones, an ex-lawyer and a very entertaining man, and the box seat by him was a much sought-after privilege. The horses were changed about every 12 miles. The moment the coach stopped the horses were taken out by one set of ostlers, and instantly the fresh horses, already harnessed, each with an ostler at his head, were buckled into their places, the reins were tossed up to the coachman who caught them across his whip and off they scampered full tilt. The time taken for this operation was counted in seconds. This coach, the wonder of the day, ran till the railways superseded it. Before it was established it was necessary to start the day and to sleep on the way, either in the coach or in a hostel. People then went to Taunton to join the coach. The system of turnpike gates was then universal, and remained for many years.

The writer goes on to mention her first railway journey which she made from Bath, having travelled there by the same Swiftsure coach which had been forced to adjust its operation to recognise the westward progress of the infant Great Western Railway.

Increasingly the former coaches with their romantic names, proud reputations and spirited driving had to yield to the railway age. Despite the glamour history has invested in stage and mail coach travel, it was never an easy option, especially in bad weather. Swiftsure may have been a special case, but coach mishaps were commonplace, with horses stumbling, lost wheels causing overturning and even outside passengers decapitated by archways or freezing to death on their exposed and precarious high perch.

T

TREADMILL AND OAKUM PICKING

Anyone convicted and sentenced to hard labour in Somerset at the beginning of the nineteenth century could expect a hard time. The punishment was intended to discourage reoffending and hard labour was exactly what it said. Oakum picking, for example, involved unravelling the strands of old rope, with the cleaner fibres being used to create new ropes or to stuff bolsters or mattresses. Much of the rope might be tarred and unpicking this was an even nastier job, with the end product utilised for caulking ships' timbers. An output of three pounds a day was expected, although often not achieved

Invented in its prison form in 1818, the treadmill or treadwheel was an even worse form of punishment and one which would exhaust even the fittest of men. At various times, there were treadmills in the prisons at Bath, Wilton and Shepton Mallet. Built locally by Stothert & Pitt, the one at Shepton Mallet comprised four huge drums, each with twenty-four 'steps' and accommodating ten prisoners, who were expected to rotate the wheel once every thirty seconds. A reserve of men was used by the turnkey to replace anyone unable to continue. A short rest was permitted on-site once an hour, but by the end of his day a new prisoner might find he had climbed the equivalent of a decent-sized mountain. The Shepton Mallet treadmill drove a shaft which powered a corn mill outside the prison wall; some of its output came back inside to feed the inmates and some was sold to local bakeries.

Those sentenced to hard labour for less than fourteen days had to do ten hours of oakum picking a day and were only allowed to leave their cells to attend chapel. The men with longer sentences were divided into two classes, both of which had to work for ten hours daily. The hardest toil fell on first class prisoners who, initially, had to spend eight of the ten hours on back breaking tasks including the treadmill and stone breaking. Prisoners in the second class spent their ten hours on slightly less physical work, in which the painful business of oakum picking was interspersed with things like mat-making as their sentence progressed. Wilton earned significant sums from its milling and stone breaking, but Shepton Mallet sometimes had to buy in loads of stone for breaking up in the twenty-two special stalls there.

The severity of the prison work began to decrease after the third month of incarceration, a point which also marked the privilege of sleeping on a mattress instead of a plank bed. Encouragement to be industrious and of good conduct came from a marks system which governed an inmate's progress from the starting Class 1 to Class 6. A daily good point represented one step towards the number required for moving to a higher class, with the work getting easier as progress was made and privileges like secular books and writing materials being granted.

The diet for prisoners increased in quantity the longer they served and the higher the class they achieved. Bread and gruel were the normal fare for breakfast and supper, the standard gruel using 'course Scotch oatmeal, with salt' being improved with an ounce of molasses for prisoners in the higher classes. The main meal of the day was dinner, when bread, cheese, potatoes, soup, suet pudding and Indian-meal pudding appeared in various permutations depending on the day of the week. The higher-grade prisoners had beef instead of pudding on Mondays and Fridays, with the stock left over going into the soup for the following day. Such extras were also provided for 'Male prisoners at Hard Labour, at Treadwheel, Crank, Flax and Rope Beating, and women employed in the laundry or other laborious occupation.'

Time.	Class	Hard Labor, 1st Class.	Hard labor, 2nd class	Employment.
1st week	1	8 hours Tread Wheel, Crank, or Stonebreaking, and 2 hours Oakum Picking.	10 hours Oakum Picking	10 hours Oakum Picking, 2 hours in the open air
Remainder of 1st month	2	8 hours Tread Wheel, Crank, or Stonebreaking, and 2 hours Oakum Picking.	10 hours Oakum Picking	10 hours Oakum Picking, 2 hours in the open air
2nd & 3rd month	3	8 hours Tread Wheel, Crank, or Stonebreaking, and 2 hours Oakum Picking.	10 hours Oakum Picking	2 hours Oakum Picking, and 8 hours Industrial Labor
4th, 5th & 6th month	4	6 hours Tread Wheel, Crank, or Stonebreaking, and 4 hours other labor.	6 hours Oakum Picking, and 4 hours other labor	10 hours Industrial Labor or other employment
7th to 12th month inclusive	5	4 hours Tread Wheel, Crank, or Stonebreaking, and 6 hours other labor.	4 hours Oakum Picking, and 6 hours other labor	10 hours Industrial Labor or other employment
Remainder of Sentence	6	2 hours Tread Wheel, Crank, or Stonebreaking, and 8 hours other labor.	2 hours Oakum Picking, and 8 hours other labor	10 hours Industrial Labor or other employment

The 'Labor Table' in use at Wilton and Shepton Mallet gaols.

In the mid-nineteenth century prisons and prison life began to change, influenced by reformers like Elizabeth Fry. Opened in 1842, Pentonville became the model for imprisonment, with the label penitentiary signalling an increased emphasis on reform. Then, in 1877, all prisons became a national responsibility and while hard labour continued, the severity of its application began to diminish.

TRUMPETER'S TALE

The Second World War was not the only example of the main hostilities being preceded by a peculiar period labelled 'the phoney war'. It happened too in the English Civil War in the months between Parliament passing the Militia Ordinance in March 1642 and King Charles I raising his standard at Nottingham in the August of that year. This was a period when attitudes on each side were hardening and increasing effort was being put into gathering moral and practical support for the respective causes. In Somerset, Colonels Popham and Strode were busy gathering the local militia forces to the Parliamentary cause, while the Marquis of Hertford was summoning those loyal to the monarch at Bath and then, more successfully, at Wells.

On the first day of August a minor skirmish took place between the two sides in the streets of Shepton Mallet, with the Royalists quick to send in reinforcements under Sir Ralph Hopton. Meanwhile, Parliamentary stalwart John Pym was hurrying from Somerton towards Street with a force of some 600 new recruits, but they were ambushed at the foot of Walton Hill and achieved the sad immortality of yielding the first serious casualties of the war. Sir John Stawell's hidden Royalist troopers opened fire from their cover in the woods, with his horsemen then riding into the shocked lines of the enemy with devastating effect.

The celebration of the Royalist victory at Marshall's Elm was short-lived, for their Wells garrison was soon to be encouraged to withdraw to Sherborne Castle by another engagement, which a Roundhead trumpeter describes in the elaborated language of the period:

> Having arrived at my journey end to Taunton-Deane, under the command of Lieutenant Howard, with whom I am entertained Trumpeter to a Troop of Horse, the next day I intended (my duty binding me thereto) to take my horse and ride to Wells, to my Father's; to which end I went to my Captaine, and told him my intent, withall desiring his licence for some days; who told me that he would go along with me to Wells, for it was in great distresse, the Cavaliers having made it their randevouz, and used several rigorous oppressions against those that did in any way oppose them.
>
> Wherefore he immediately caused me to sound my Trumpet through Taunton-Deane; a Corporall giving notice that it was his desire that all Gentlemen or others

This engraving, *View of the City of Wells from the S.E.* by J.C.Varrall, was prepared for a book *Picturesque Antiquities of English Cities* published by Longman in 1830. The original drawing would have been made at the top of Tor Hill, one of the vantage points used by the Parliamentary artillery in 1642.

that were possest of any Horse, or Horse-man's Armes, should instantly put themselves into a Posture of Defence, and repaire to him. Which was speedily effected, for within three hours there were with my Captaine's owne Horses, and those that were sent in, an hundred and twenty. Which being put in order by Lieutenant Howard, we immediately marched upon Wells, where being arrived we found the Countrey all in Armes, and the Towne besieged on every side.

On the hill coming off Mendip from Bristow-ward, there was Sir Francis Popham and Sir Edward Hungerford, with five thousand armed men, and two pieces of Ordnance, which were mounted against the Bishop's Pallace. Between Glastenbury and Wells there was Sir Edward Gainton and Sir John Horner, with eight thousand men or thereabouts. On the hill on the East side (Tor Hill?) between Skipton Mallard and Wells, there was Master Pine, Master Cole and Master Strowd, with three thousand more, and two Peeces which they had mounted to command any part of town, where occasion should require.

Wherefore Sir Edward Hungerford, after a courteous welcome, entreated us to make a good passage from Wells, On the North-east of the Towne, which goes up to the Downes to meet the Skipton Mallet roade, which leads to Bristowe, which was accordingly performed by us; the Army being in order, Sir Francis Popham caused some shots to be made from Mendip Hill against the Bishop's Pallace which, by reason of the strength thereof, they had made their Quarters, it being a place of considerable strength and moted round about.

Nevertheless the report of our Ordnance made the Cavaliers bestirred themselves, see themselves surrounded by the Country, and knowing the Towne was no place of strength or security either to oppose us, or to secure themselves from us, wherefore they made as if they intended to force a passage towards Glastenbury, which caused all our parties of foot to presse up to secure those passages, which they seeing, with their utmost speed at a passage betweene the wood and us, trooped out upon us fronting boldly, which they well might, they being in number much greater and more experienced men, both in Horsemanship, and use of Arms, our men being raw, untutored and unexperienced in the uses of Armes and Horsemanship, our Foote likewise being so far behind, by reason of the mistake, that it was impossible to reach them, besides our Ordnance which was planted on the Hill, lying so high, could not command them, they keeping just under the bottom of the said Hill, being sheltered by the Wood.

Nevertheless, our Captaine (neither esteeming their number, or weighing the danger that might happen by his attempting to intercept a Party so strong, and pursued by almost inevitable ruine and perpetual destruction) gave command that wee should give Fire upon them, which was with unexpected alacrity, and undaunted courage performed. They did the like at us, but such their haste was, that they could not stay to see the execution, nor doe we know whether we did against them, for it was not policie to pursue them, they having the greater number. Besides, had wee engaged ourselves beyond the bounds or succour of our Forces, wee might have been cut off, and they had cause to laugh at our destruction. The Towne being thus quit of them, wee drew our Forces in, where wee were entertained with great joy.

U

UNCLEAN! UNCLEAN!

Although leprosy existed here well before the Crusades, the rapid spread of the disease is often attributed to Crusaders returning from what we now call the Middle East. Certainly the nobles and fighting men who came back from these conflicts brought back with them many eastern influences which profoundly affected almost every aspect of home life – dress, food and drink, buildings, furnishings and the like. Unfortunately, leprosy may have been among their imports, for the pattern of leprosy certainly followed a similar timescale to that of the Crusades. The age-old disease gradually spread to all classes in the eleventh century, was widespread over the next 200 years and then declined slowly but steadily from the later fourteenth century.

Leprosy was a terrible malady, greatly feared and affecting all but the most remote parts of the country. It was a chronic condition in which bacteria attacked the nerves and skin, and those who contracted the disease could expect terrible blotches and other deformities leading, in the advanced stages, to paralysis, the loss of extremities, blindness and even death. Despite the existence of over 200 hospitals for lepers, only soothing treatments were available and the lot of the afflicted was miserable indeed. The county of Somerset was not immune from this terrible visitation.

Leper hospitals were usually known as a Spital or Lazar House, the former an abbreviation of hospital and the latter an acknowledgement of the lepers' patron saint, Lazarus. They were mostly dedicated to St Margaret, run by the monasteries and funded by grants and charitable donations which bishops encouraged by the offer of indulgences. In Somerset, the Hospital of St Margaret was established for Taunton in the twelfth century. It came under royal protection and received numerous ecclesiastical bequests in the next centuries, with Canon Bruton adding his 20*s* to the list in 1417 and the Taunton lazar house again featuring in a will of 1537. By 1548, the effects of the Reformation had adversely affected the finances of the establishment and it was forced to make 'humble peticon for augmentation of lyving'. By 1612 there was a change of use and the building became an almshouse, reflecting the decline in leprosy.

Slightly later than the Taunton foundation, which was located well outside the town at East Reach, came such hospitals at Ilchester and Langport, the latter granted a brief in 1310 by Bishop Drokensfeld, authorising the collection of alms within his diocese. The one at Bridgwater, dedicated to St Giles, was not so well endowed. Bedminster and Bath also cared for their lepers. The legendary founder of the latter, Prince Bladud, himself had suffered from leprosy and the city had both a leper hospital and a small bathing facility to enable sufferers to access the same curative waters Bladud was supposed to have discovered. Dating from early in the thirteenth century, this hospital was strategically sited near the Fosse Way in order to solicit alms from travellers and prevent lepers from entering the city.

As if it was not bad enough to suffer from such a debilitating condition, lepers had other crosses to bear. The disease was widely held to be a punishment for sin on the part of the sufferer, especially carnal behaviour, and the leper hospitals run by religious orders tended to reflect this with a great deal of prayer and fasting in their regimes. Leprosy was widely believed to be an airborne infection, and so lepers were required to endure isolation and privation in addition to their other troubles.

Although lepers were not compelled to enter lazar houses, all sorts of local laws governing their situation began to emerge. The parish priest or a special jury could examine someone believed to be infected and declare them 'secluded'. The unfortunate person was then banned from entry to churches, markets and other such places where large numbers of people gathered. Contact was limited. If a leper met someone in the open air, convention only permitted a conversation to take place if the healthy person stood upwind of the leper. The latter had to wear a uniform of sorts, usually a distinctive cloak, hood and overshoes for men and a double black veil for women, all designed to screen their unsightliness. All this was provided, along with a bell or clapper which had to be used to ensure their presence was not overlooked. In some cases a self-contained dwelling would be arranged, complete with furnishings and its own well.

Lepers were allowed to beg outside the town gates, although this activity was later restricted and they were sometimes compelled to use licensed proctors for this purpose. Edward III excluded lepers from his capital in 1346. There were also constraints on the property and other rights of lepers, and if it had not been for the caring work of the monasteries and the better local communities, they would have had little to ease their condition.

In the fifteenth century, Hugh, Bishop of Lincoln, left three marks to each of the leper hospitals at Selwood, Bath and Ilchester. This enlightened prelate subscribed to a more generous view of leprosy, in which it was believed that the torment suffered on earth would permit lepers direct entry to heaven without enduring further agony in purgatory. He observed, 'the more deformed their bodies, the brighter shone their souls; and the greater their suffering, the more certain they were of salvation.' Fortunately, the awful disease was then on the wane.

UNREST AND COMMOTION

Rioting and civil commotion are not generally associated with essentially rural counties like Somerset, but most areas have had a taste of civil unrest at one time or another. Local issues involving religion or high-handed action by the gentry sparked most of the earlier examples in Somerset, while the later centuries saw the emergence of more complex cases and causes. Shortages and the high cost of food which followed poor harvests provoked desperation among hungry men, with familiar fears also surfacing when jobs seemed to be threatened by changes such as the introduction of machinery. Miners, because of their large and concentrated grouping, were a major factor in some of these cases, especially in opposition to turnpikes and in the ongoing struggle to improve wages and conditions. Politics, of course, frequently aroused strong feelings and, sometimes, strong action.

Rioting occurred in Frome in 1757 when the distress resulting from the high price of corn was affecting the whole of the country. On 5 April about 200 colliers started one of the mills working and then planned to burn it down, but the miller managed to bribe them to leave. In the following month, desperation and the feeling that millers were profiting from their plight led to violent attacks on several mills along the river at Frome. This time, things got out of hand at one mill where the miners were met by an armed miller and his men, and two people were killed. Two more were wounded before two companies of Wolfe's Regiment arrived to break up the conflict. There was one innocent victim; a young boy who had joined the crowd out of curiosity and was shot in the throat.

Attacks on farm barns and the theft of corn occurred several times in the sixteenth century. In 1753 there was more collective action when miners took matters into their own hands, with a huge crowd of them taking over Shepton Mallet market and setting their own price for the sale of corn.

Widespread national dissatisfaction appeared again after the poor harvest of 1795, and yet again in 1799. By this time the country was at war with France, which affected grain imports; it also had a government reluctant to interfere with market forces. The militia sent to maintain order were loath to act against their suffering countrymen, who had fixed their immediate anger on farmers, millers and merchants. Forestallers, who bought grain wherever they could obtain it at a reasonable price and then sold it at a great profit, were also a prime target.

Hunger and poverty inexorably led to widespread malnourishment and desperation and, in turn, to an understandable frustration which only found relief in physical and often angry expression. Inevitably, on some occasions this escalated into open and bloody conflict. At Beckington in 1766, for example, a miller's defence of his property against a hungry and pitiable mob led to one death and several woundings.

A colourful and entirely more peaceful market place at Shepton Mallet than when it was taken over by angry miners in 1753.

In other, earlier confrontations there were riots against disafforestation action by the Bishop of Bath & Wells back in 1338 and, 300 years later, against attempts to implement a royal injunction requiring communion tables to be railed off. At Beckington the churchwardens' appeal to the Court of Arches on this issue failed in the face of royal intervention, and the petitioners were threatened with both civil conviction and religious excommunication. Only the humiliation of public submission to the bishop saved them.

In 1349 Bath & Wells' bishop was besieged by an angry mob during his visit to a church in Yeovil. They were labelled as 'sons of perdition', but may just have been driven to rash expression by the terror of the worst period of the Black Death plague. The unfortunate cleric was rescued after involuntary overnight confinement, and made the offenders undertake public penance for their actions.

Turnpikes engendered a lot of hostility in their early days; local people were frequently nervous of change and any restrictions on the traditional ways. South of Bristol in 1749, several gates were attacked by a mob, mostly armed with weapons, some dressed in women's clothes, others carrying homemade flags or beating a drum, all noisy and determined to destroy what they saw as a threat. The gate on the Ashton road was, in fact, destroyed on three occasions.

Reaction to new machinery affected Shepton Mallet in 1776, when cloth workers destroyed several of the new machines which had been installed to do their work more quickly and cheaply. In another confrontation, Hardisty's Mill was burned down in similar action.

The great protest action surrounding the Parliamentary reform changes at the beginning of the 1830s not only included the notable rioting in Bristol, but embraced an orgy of rick-burning and destruction of threshing machines in 1831. That winter saw a most serious riot at Wells, with such devastation caused to the bishop's palace that he later received over £8,000 in compensation.

The nineteenth century also witnessed action by the Radstock miners in 1830, on strike in an effort to improve their lot. Later, in Nailsea, a great deal of damage was done when, after six weeks of strike action, some of the striking men returned to their workplace, thereby incurring the angry vengeance of their workmates. At the time, Nailsea had but one constable who found himself unsupported by the special constables who had been sworn in, and quite powerless to act. With a salary of only £1 a week, he could hardly be blamed!

UNUSUAL PROCEDURE

An especially unusual event occurred in the Puxton area in the years before the Enclosure Act. Quite a large portion of the adjacent moors was common land and, in the case of the East and West Dolmoors (or Dolemoors), was let annually for grazing in forty lots of one acre. These lots would have had a differing appeal to prospective users by reasons of tradition, quality and convenience, and a somewhat peculiar method was used to ensure that the allocation between those eligible was fair and such as to avoid resentment.

Accounts of the event differ slightly and the format may well have varied over the years, but it seems that interested parties were first summoned by bell to Puxton Church, where they could check the measuring chain on display. This was then taken out onto the moors so that the correct distance between the posts separating the various lots could be verified. The lots were distinguished by means of a simple diagram cut into the turf, probably refreshed annually.

The letting procedure involved a number of apples, with marks corresponding to those on the turf, being placed in a bag and then drawn out by a lad and handed at random to each of the hopefuls. By comparing the symbol on the apple with that on the plot, each user knew where his grazing acre lay. Quite possibly some exchanges and 'horse trading' followed, but there was no basis for quarrelling with such a simple but effective allocation.

However, the business was not over yet, for a candle auction then took place at the Dolmoor overseer's house for a separate plot of four acres known as the Out Drift, the proceeds from this being intended for the expenses of posts, gates and other items used to maintain the Dolmoors. It was also designed to

Beyond the graveyard of the tiny church of Holy Saviour at Puxton lies the moorland once let annually in a curious ritual. Parts of the church, now a carefully preserved treasure, date back to the twelfth century.

pay for the bread, butter, cheese, ale and tobacco consumed at the annual feast which climaxed the whole proceedings. The auction took place in silence so that overt rigging was avoided, and each bidder was required to lay down a token shilling as he made his bid, which was then retrieved if he was outbid. When the candle flame finally trembled to extinction, the last bid was deemed successful, the money handed over and a large proportion of it then quickly consumed in the social jollity which rounded off the occasion.

V

VICTIM FIGHTS BACK

There was high drama in Congresbury in the late afternoon of 21 October 1830. A farmer, Charles Capell Hardwicke, had set out for Bristol market earlier in the day and was on his way home after successfully concluding his business there. In his saddle bags was £500 in gold, a product of the day's enterprise, and he was greatly looking forward to getting it and himself safely back to his home on the heath. But the reality proved vastly different.

Hardwicke was overtaken on the road by another horseman, who proved to be a distant relative, one Richard Hewlett. Whether there was bad blood between the two or some violent quarrel arose is not known, but something prompted Hewlett to draw a pistol and fire at his companion from close range. He could not miss, and the ball struck Hardwicke in the shoulder. Failing in his attempted murder, the assassin galloped away towards the centre of the village with a shocked, but not immobilised farmer in pursuit.

The memorial to brave farmer Charles Hardwicke in Congresbury churchyard.

The engagement between the two resumed on the bridge over the Yeo with each combatant trying to throw the other off his horse and Hewlett abandoning a second pistol in favour of a dagger housed in his cane. Even then he could not overcome the angry Hardwicke, despite stabbing him in the side.

So fierce was the resistance of his intended victim that Hewlett's courage failed and he fled back towards the heath with Hardwicke in hot pursuit. The chase continued in the dusk for 1 mile until the fleeing horse was startled by the lights of an approaching cart and fell, throwing its rider. Following closely, his angry pursuer fell over the fallen Hewlett and his horse and, despite his loss of blood, managed to pin down the man who had so violently interrupted his homeward journey.

The horrific events had been noticed and help appeared to secure Hewlett and detain him for eventual trial at the Assizes. His intended victim was taken, exhausted and bleeding, to the Ship & Castle to receive medical attention, but hovered between life and death for some time. 'The full sentence of the law' was passed on the dreadful assassin for 'attempted murder and highway robbery' and he subsequently paid the ultimate price for his deeds at Ilchester Gaol.

Some twenty-two years after his death at Hutton in 1849, a subscription was launched to raise money for a memorial record of the courage Hardwicke displayed in the 1830 incident and this remains, proud and well cared for, in the churchyard at Congresbury.

W

WELLINGTON MONUMENT

Born in Dublin in 1769, Arthur Wellesley proved his prowess as a military commander in Flanders, India, the Iberian Peninsula, France, and ultimately, the iconic Battle of Waterloo. His ongoing successes saw him knighted, made a viscount, a marquis and eventually a duke. Less than deliberately, it seems, he chose to be Duke of Wellington to go along with the £100,000 awarded to him by a grateful Parliament for outlay on land and property. In the process he also became Wellington's lord of the manor.

Following the victory at Waterloo, which brought an end to the long years of the Napoleonic wars, there was general euphoria throughout the country. The gentry of Wellington were not immune, and after news of the decisive battle became widely known, opened a subscription to provide a memorial to Wellesley's achievements. Their designer and architect planned to raise a square column topped by a massive statue in cast iron, with cannons from Waterloo around the base and three cottages for veterans of that bloody conflict. The intention was also to have an annual celebration on 18 June, the battle anniversary, to be known as 'The Wake of Waterloo'.

The Wellington monument.

A foundation stone was laid in 1817, but the Waterloo triumph began to lose its impact and the subscriptions just did not meet expectations, despite a visit from Wellington himself in 1819. For a long time the construction remained in a part-built state until a simpler design permitted its eventual completion in 1854.

Restored by public subscription in 1892 and now cared for by the National Trust, the 175ft high triangular column of the Wellington Monument stands on a hilltop, not far from the town itself, and visible to every motorist on the M5 motorway. From the top of the 235 narrow stairs, there are magnificent views across the surrounding Blackdown Hills and towards the Brendons and Exmoor.

WHITPOT AND FURMITY

Many traditional foods and dishes are well-known in and beyond the county. Bath buns, Bath Olivers and Cheddar cheese are notable food examples. Other once well-loved items have largely disappeared from our tables. Two Bath examples are Bath chaps, delicate parts of a young pig's head cured in sweet pickle, and Bath polony, a smaller and more delicate version of the Continental polony.

Whitpot and Furmity are alternative names for the same dish. As Furmity, it had a very ancient international origin and was much enjoyed in Somerset, especially on Mothering Sunday and various saint's days. The principal ingredients were wheat, currants and spices boiled in milk, with raisins forming Somerset's special extra ingredient. An old recipe advises:

> Take half a pint of wheat, half a pound of raisins, half a pound of currants and half a gallon of milk. Boil the wheat in water until quite tender the day before making the furmity; boil the raisins and currants separately. Next day put on the milk and bring nearly to the boil, add the wheat and let it cook thoroughly, then add the raisins and currants, and allow to simmer for three hours or more. Add sugar or spice and serve in cups or basins.

This concoction, also called Whitpit or Frumenty, was also eaten at the once frequent meetings of various men's clubs, where it was a regular favourite.

A favourite for the farmhouse kitchen meal for a large family was crowdy pie. It was really more of a pasty and was made by placing the ingredients, mainly apples, bacon and onions, on rolled-out pastry and then bringing the edges together ready for baking in the oven. Often the pie would be enormous, and each family tended to have its own special version created by whatever additional ingredients they favoured.

In West Somerset, some areas had their own variation of the crowdy pie theme, one very old alternative using cormorants or pigeons as the main ingredient.

When young pigeons, known as squabs, were used, the result was usually better known as squab pie. Kingsley, writing about this version in another part of the country, rather startling referred to its aroma as 'a delicate odour of mingled guano and polecat'!

Crowdy pie may largely have disappeared, but another old dish, elver cakes, is still eaten and enjoyed. On the first high tides of spring, huge numbers of tiny young eels head up the Somerset rivers to be caught at night by experts wielding a hoop with a canvas bag attached, attracting the young eels by the light of a lantern or torch. The elver catch is boiled, pressed into small, round containers and then sliced to create small pancakes for frying.

For the thirsty, Somerset cider has always had a special place in the county, especially for those whose working life was hot and wearisome. Combinations of cider with ale seem often to have been known as Lamb's Wool, with the name having a tenuous connection with the blessing of the apple on La Mas Ubhal, the Day of the Apple. Lamb's Wool was the drink of the day for All Hallows' Eve and was compounded of ale, nutmeg, toast, sugar and roasted apples. No doubt it was not abandoned the rest of the year!

Still cooked in Somerset are Watchet fig pie and Dunster's whortleberry pie. Stogursey celery soup provides warmth on cold days and many a family have eaten and enjoyed a Somerset oggie pasty based on the home-reared and slaughtered pig. Stowey apple pudding, or Somerset pudding with alternate layers of apple and sponge, would also taste good, especially topped with cider sauce.

WIFE FOR SALE

Seemingly, it has always been easier to get into a marriage than to get out of one. Provided there were no complications or objections, the established church would normally oblige a man and woman who wished to marry. Even if there were, a variety of itinerant preachers and charlatans were to be found who would offer spurious credentials and readily join a couple in supposed wedlock for a suitable fee. Some form of simple contract could also validate a union.

Getting out of a marriage was a completely different matter. There were options in common law, ecclesiastical courts and by Act of Parliament, but they were limited and only the very wealthy could afford them. The position did begin to change with the passing of the Matrimonial Causes Act of 1857, but only slowly, and ordinary folk could do little to end a broken relationship before that.

Somehow, this predicament gave birth to a somewhat unusual custom dating back at least to the seventeenth century and probably earlier, one example occurring in 1552. The custom involved a husband offering his wife for sale in much the same way that prize animals were auctioned at market; possibly owing something to that process. In essence, the offer of a wife for sale had to take place in a market square or other public area, the wife had to be led in with a halter around her neck and a public official or other respected person had to witness the affair. If required, the husband would purchase a market toll ticket and hand it in to the purchaser as proof of ownership.

Thomas Hardy recorded wife-selling examples in his 'notebook' and featured the process early in his well-known novel *The Mayor of Casterbridge*. Somerset was not excluded from the practice which, though extremely unsavoury by today's standards, could, in its time, just represent a slightly bizarre way of accommodating the wishes of both the parties involved. Usually the marriage would already have foundered and the woman be seeking a union with another man.

Several examples of Somerset wife-selling occurred in the nineteenth century, including the sale of one Lizzie Taff in the centre of Chard in 1801. Thirty-eight years later, the following report appeared in the *Chard Union Gazette* and refers to an apparent second example in the same year:

> Marriage Extraordinary
>
> The first marriage ceremony performed in Chard Church by the present officiating minister, the Rev. W. Whitehead Jun, was under circumstances which do not every day occur; the parties were a man named Morris, and a woman named Phillips, who have lived together upwards of 38 years in perfect amity and had a large family, but delayed their approach to the hymeneal altar till within the last few days; the woman it appears had been married to a man named Phillips, by whom she was sold 38 years ago for half-a crown to the person who has just made her his wife, but with whom she has lived ever since; her real husband having died about two months ago, she seems to have entered into the spirit of the old adage, 'better late than never' and cleared her conscience by entering into the 'holy state'.

In fact, the newspaper appears to have got its dates wrong with the 'sale' actually taking place in 1805. The parties were Joseph Phelps, aka Phillips, and Elizabeth Christopher. Their marriage at Chaffcombe in January 1803 only lasted long enough for them to have a son before Joseph took his worldly goods and left for a new location at Chatworth, Chard. By the end of 1804 Elizabeth had moved in with one Henry Morris in another part of Chard and was 'sold' to him by auction in 1805 for half-a-crown. Between this event and the church marriage in 1839, two more children were born, but Elizabeth could not say who the father was when she later claimed an allowance while Henry was in the militia, as the parties involved seemed to have remained on remarkably good terms!

In a rather unusual example on the Somerset border, a basket of gingerbread was included in the sale. The occasion was the Tuesday market in Stalbridge in April 1814 and the vendor Thomas Tuffen of Henstridge. He and his wife regularly attended local fairs and market to sell gingerbread, which they doubtless made in their own home. The purchaser was local sawyer, Joseph Cairns, who led the lady back to his home, and probably helped himself to a sample from the basket of gingerbread which formed part of his bargain.

The heart of Chard where Lizzie Taff featured in one of at least two wife-selling incidents in the town.

After seven years of marriage, Simon Mitchell of Taunton 'sold' his wife Sarah to James Larcombe of Curry Rivel for two sovereigns around the year 1830. James was fifteen years older than his new 'bride', but the couple settled down in Westover, Langport where James made a living as a shoemaker, and the two got on well enough to produce ten children, all taking the Mitchell surname. Sadly, age and poverty eventually overtook James and Sarah, with him being recorded as a pauper and she eking out a living as a washerwoman in Taunton, the place of her legal husband's official settlement. A couple of years after this sale, another shoemaker 'bought' the wife of labourer Charles Pearce at Buckland, near Frome, for £5.

The sums paid in the various wife-selling incidents varied, but rose steadily over the years. Where the sale was merely a formality ratifying an agreement between the parties, the amount involved might be just a few pence or well under one pound. In a more genuine auction the price could be higher. Hardy settled on a sum of 5 guineas for Michael Henchard's sale in *The Mayor of Casterbridge*, but a wife sold at the Bell Inn, Farmborough near Bath commanded only a gallon of beer!

As the nineteenth century progressed, the number of wife-selling cases declined, but not before a curious example came to light in a Wincanton court action around 1869. When a baker sued a Mrs Newport for payment for bread he had supplied, it came out that the lady in question had been on her own ever since her husband had led her to Shepton market to be sold. There she had been bought by her own father for no less than £500 and given an allowance of 10*s* a week to compensate for the flight of her husband.

Referring to a wife-sale in St Thomas Market, Bristol a contemporary verse observed:

Come all you kind husbands who have scolding wives,
Who thro' living together are tired of your lives,
If you cannot persuade her nor good natur'd make her,
Place rope round her neck & to market pray take her.

Should any one bid, when she's offered for sale,
Let her go for a trifle lest she should get stale,
If sixpence be offer'd, & that's all can be had,
Let her go for the same rather than keep a lot bad.

Come all jolly neighbours, come dance sing & play,
Away to the wedding where we intend to drink tea;
All the world assembles, the young and the old,
For to see this fair beauty, as we have been told.

Here's success to this couple to keep up the fun,
May bumpers go round at the birth of a son;
Long life to them both, and in peace & content
May their days and their nights for ever be spent.

Y

YABLE AND VUDDLES

Special words peculiar to a locality are one of the delights of the English language, however frustrating they may be to those trying to learn it. Many such words have, sadly, slipped away into the mists of time and memory; something of a shame, for they mostly have a novelty and richness that is unmatched by their modern usurpers. Somerset is no exception in this matter.

In some cases the origin of special words is fairly obvious. 'Romancing' used to mean delirious is clear enough, while 'frappish' for cross may have its roots in the French verb frapper. 'Yable' meaning able, and 'vuddles' indicating pampering are less clear, unless the latter is a baby talk alternative to cuddles.

Trades always contribute to the special language vocabulary. From the Radstock coalfield area of the county comes 'gug' for the inclined tramways used to move tubs of coal, while 'hudge' was one of the iron buckets used in the mines. The pit itself was a 'carl-pet' which was very close to its more proper enunciation, whereas 'boitle' for a heavy wooden hammer is rather obscure in origin.

In the sphere of health and well-being being, peevish or restless would be labelled 'twiley', but 'sprach' just meant rather the opposite (quick or lively). Good health attracted the adjective 'trigg' or the description 'pure', but to 'pitch away', or grow thin, and then catch the 'grief-that-goes-about' (otherwise known as typhoid), could eventually turn one into an 'attomy', or a skeleton! To stay well it was best to avoid things 'daddicky' meaning decayed or rotten and anything 'blatchy' meaning dirty, both words one did not really want to hear.

Wild creatures might have to be hunted and killed in the course of protecting crops or providing for the table, but they have also attracted an interest and affection that has given them their own share of special but unusual words, often quite localised in use. In East Somerset moles, for example, were 'moby-warps', but elsewhere they might be 'wants'. In West Somerset polecats were 'fitchets' and in other places 'feeches' or 'fetchegs'. Such varying geographical treatment was also accorded to bullfinches which could be either 'whoops' or 'red hoops'. Chaffinches were rather charmingly known as 'twinks'.

Among the other examples of this special language are:

A-slatt	musically out of tune
Blowth	blossom
Caddle	a mess, muddle or confusion
Dudder	confuse
Dumping and dreshing	children playing and messing about
Fowt	fetched
Gout	a drain
Helt	weight
Junks	feasts or jollification
Larniger or lamiger	cripple
Leasing	gleaning
Neighboury	visit
Rere	early
Spluth	riot or commotion
Twinny	fright
Tuttie	nosegay or bunch of flowers
Warsley	wrestle
Whoe	care for; look after.

YEOVIL RAILWAY RIVALRY

In the middle of the nineteenth century Yeovil found itself involved in a major territorial battle between the emerging broad-gauge railway empire of the Great Western Railway and that of its narrow gauge London & South Western Railway rival. Both companies had achieved their first ambitions and were now keen on expansion, with Exeter as a prime target. Devon had originally seemed certain to be the secure province of the GWR, for its associated Bristol & Exeter Railway had already opened as far as Bridgwater by 1841 to extend the broad-gauge route from London via Bristol. Broad gauge services to Exeter soon followed.

The next few years featured a succession of discussions, agreements, disagreements and new expansion plans relating to the South Somerset and Dorset areas, including one for a broad-gauge B&E branch line to Yeovil. In Parliamentary sessions in 1846, 1847 and 1848 an incredible amount of time was spent in considering the proposals put forward by the big companies and their satellites. The estimated cost of these years of argument was put at over £300,000. One mammoth hearing in Parliament in 1847 lasted fifty-three days, and small fortunes were made by various legal, engineering and surveying experts who were paid considerable sums to support one or other side of the debate and rubbish the assertions of the rival schemes.

These proceedings eventually authorised a number of new routes which offered Yeovil hopes of a railway connection, but for the time being little actually happened. Not only had the Parliamentary expenses taxed the companies heavily, but the whole mania of railway speculation had subsided, dividends were down and capital was not to be had. Lack of funds hit work on the routes already authorised and underway, with activity coming to a halt on the approach to Salisbury, beyond Westbury on the GWR line from Thingley Junction to Weymouth, and on the branch line from Taunton to Yeovil, which stalled at Martock for four years.

The 1850s started badly; Yeovil seemed no nearer to getting the railway access that would bring badly needed stimulation to its economy. Certainly an independent Salisbury & Yeovil scheme had been among the bright prospects of 1848, but the L&SW kept having lively boardroom battles over whether or not to support it, a situation which continued until Parliament insisted that the larger company honoured its commitment to get to Exeter and stipulated severe penalties for any failure to do so.

The Wilts, Somerset & Weymouth scheme authorised back in 1845 had fared no better than the others in reaching Yeovil. It had been taken over by the GWR in 1850, but that company had its own financial problems and was even taken to court in an attempt to get the project completed. It put up a successful defence and thus the century moved into its second half with the three railway schemes vital to Yeovil still no more than part-filled aspirations.

The prospect of better communications did seem to have improved with the arrival of the first broad-gauge B&E trains to serve Yeovil on 1 October 1853. These trains from Taunton via Durston initially terminated at a station at Hendford, on the outskirts of the town, but were extended through to Pen Mill station, on the Weymouth route, on 2 February 1857. The Weymouth route had moved forward from Frome to Yeovil on 1 September 1856 and reached Weymouth four months later. Then, on 1 June 1860, the route from London via Salisbury brought Yeovil its third train service, with the extension to Exeter following quickly on 19 July. The L&SW line trains to Yeovil used a connection to Hendford for a short time until Yeovil Junction station was ready on the main line. Subsequently, a joint and more central station, Yeovil Town, was opened on 1 June 1861.

Although it finally had services on three railway routes, the complexities at Yeovil were not yet at an end. It became a place of broad, narrow and mixed gauge lines and trains. Yeovil Town station, for example, had two signal boxes for each of its two users and three different sets of staff, L&SW, B&E and joint. From 1864 a special goods station had to be brought into use at Clifton Maybank, on the L&SWR line to Exeter, to handle the transport of goods between the companies and their two different gauges.

Gradually the dual gauge situation was simplified, which improved interchange at Yeovil, but the reduction of its complex railway network to just two lines and two rather inconvenient stations in the 1960s might have left a better legacy had the town not been caught up in the rivalries and uncertainties of the early railway years.

Index

Printed in Great Britain
by Amazon

53257417R00093